The True Cognoscente's Culture Test

Other books by Abbie Salny and Marvin Grosswirth

THE MENSA GENIUS QUIZ BOOK
THE MENSA GENIUS QUIZ BOOK 2

The True Cognoscente's Culture Test

You know your I.Q.— now learn your C.Q. (Culture Quotient)

Abbie Salny and Marvin Grosswirth

1817

HARPER & ROW, PUBLISHERS, New York
Cambridge, Philadelphia, San Francisco, London
Mexico City, São Paulo, Singapore, Sydney

FIRST EDITION

Designer: Gilda Hannah

Library of Congress Cataloging in Publication Data

Salny, Abbie F.
    The true cognoscente's culture test.

    1. Questions and answers. I. Grosswirth, Marvin,
1931–1984. II. Title.
AG195.S26 1984   031'.02 84-47596
ISBN 0-06-091184-0 (pbk.)

---

84 85 86 87 88 10 9 8 7 6 5 4 3 2 1

To Marilyn Grosswirth and Jerry Salny for all the right reasons

And to my mother, Edith Feinstein, who showed me the wonderful world of books —A.F.S.

Contents

The True Cognoscente's Culture Test

You, Too, Can Be a Snob

Why did we write this book? Was it to teach you to be cultured? Not at all. This is not a book that will teach anyone to be a cultured person. Culture, to paraphrase a famous saying, cannot be taught, it can only be learned.

Culture, if you are very lucky, is something you are born to and acquire by osmosis as you grow up and are exposed to it all around you. Many who are not so fortunate acquire culture by dint of hard work, ambition, and a real desire to do so. And if you are deficient in all of the above, at least you have this book.

Who decides what is culture? In this book, we did. The choices made are ours, and you may or may not agree with them, as you choose. The ultimate in culture, of course, would be to write your own book on the subject.

Naturally, there are many ways to learn to be cultured, and many mishaps along the way for those who seek to acquire this elusive ideal. A famous comedian's story sums up some of the perils and pitfalls. This tale relates the adventures of a worthy, hard-working couple, who built up a successful business in a very snobbish suburb. They were highly regarded, but they were not welcome socially, which bothered them a great deal. At last, the long-awaited day came when they were invited to a cocktail party at the home of one of the doyennes of Society (with a capital S, of course). They arrived in their party finery, and proceeded to feel extremely uncomfortable, as guests all around them discussed Mondrian, Wagner, Warhol, and Proust with equal ease. Finally, one woman said, "To my mind, it is absolutely necessary to get to know Mozart, because he is probably the greatest musician who ever lived." The couple looked at each other in distress, and the woman could stand it no longer. She said, "I agree completely. As a matter of fact, I spoke to him on the Number Five bus to the beach, only last week." This was followed by dead silence for a few moments, and the original speaker then changed the subject abruptly. The husband could barely restrain his fury, and the couple left almost immediately. On the way home, he stopped the car, turned to his wife, and said, "You idiot—why did you show your ignorance to everyone? Everybody knows the Number Five bus doesn't go to the beach!"

Of course, if that sadly uncultured woman had said

her line with a laugh, nobody would have assumed that she did not know who Mozart was. It could well have been taken for an amusing example of satire. On the other hand, she might have said nothing until the conversation turned to something with which she was familiar. In short, a shut mouth gathers no feet.

Despite all this, it is possible to acquire the tools to help bridge such embarrassing gaps. You must work hard and you must pay attention, not necessarily for the sake of learning, but just to outwit all those people who lay traps for superior individuals like yourself. You must do some reading, and you must *want* to acquire knowledge. One man who was far less educated than his wife found an ingenious solution many years ago. He had her read to him on all the long business drives they were forced to take, and he absorbed a good deal of culture that way. Tapes that can be played in your car are a modern adaptation of the same scenario.

Those who are determined to acquire culture will do it, one way or another. We have assembled these quizzes to help you, and to amuse you in the course of your self-education.

How did we decide what to include in this book? First of all, we ruled out fads. Fads are the culture of the crowd, and the cultured person is above the crowd, or ahead of the crowd. A truly cultured person pays no attention to "pop" culture, but does so in a way that does not cause others to take offense. That is, of course, unless the cultured person is dealing

with people it is entirely permissible to insult—in-
laws, for example.

We have omitted any reference to narcotics and
their use. There is no dope in this book. We don't
care how "cultured" it may be; we refuse to discuss
it. We do discuss alcohol in various guises because
being au courant with wines is not at all equivalent
to being an alcoholic, and because a knowledge of
wines, spirits, grape culture, and accompaniments to
fine food has always been considered a mark of the
truly cultured individual. Not knowing whether Sauternes is a dry wine or a sweet wine can produce
some embarrassment if you are the host or hostess at
a restaurant dinner party, or even if you are ordering
wine for your own use in a fine dining establishment.

We consider that we are offering, through the variety of subject area included in these quizzes, a
chance to acquire painlessly a large store of facts
which, rest assured, the noncultured are not likely to
know.

The first area we thought important was the field
of literature. There should be no argument that the
great written works of art, whether they are secular
or religious in origin, are part of our culture.

The second area we thought important was the
arts, especially the visual arts (painting, sculpture,
and architecture), which appear first in the text, and
later on, the performing arts, by which we meant
music, dance, and theater.

Our next category was daily living. Manners and
mores play a large role in our culture, even if they are

not always thought of as a basic part of high culture. Surely manners have always been a mark of culture, and the manners of cultured people have always been the standard by which others are measured.

Food, too, has its status position. While there are "pop" foods, as there is "pop" art and "pop" music, certain styles of dining are generally considered to be associated with culture. An epicure who enters what is considered a fine restaurant would not expect to have the table set with paper place mats and mismatched cutlery and glasses. There are certain standards that are generally accepted, and certain assumptions that are generally shared (otherwise etiquette books would not be best-sellers).

Our next area was the scientific. As C. P. Snow indicated, it is necessary to be knowledgeable in this field also to be considered truly cultured nowadays. Mathematical or scientific illiteracy is as fatal to any claim to being cultured as literary illiteracy would have been one hundred years ago.

Next, we chose famous people, places, and events that had a significant impact on the world. While we may not approve of their actions, generals and rulers have altered the course of the world for better or for worse, and must be considered in any overview of culture.

Last of all is a little "lagniappe." This is a section containing odd, unusual, and interesting bits of culture that simply defied the more orderly categories.

So go ahead. Have fun, score yourself, and then rate your cultural superiority on our C.Q. (Culture

Quotient) scale. People have been casually hinting about their high I.Q.s for years. Now you can proudly note your very own Culture Quotient on the card that we have thoughtfully provided for you at the end of this book. Good luck!

Word Wise and Otherwise: Mythology, Literature, and Legend

Anyone who claims even a nodding acquaintance with culture should have knowledge of the literature and legend of the past as well as the best sellers of today, not omitting the sacred writings of the various religions. You never know when the opportunity will arise for you to slip in a deft reference to some piece of classical literature, thereby showing your familiarity with this area of culture. In the words of the old chestnut, "Shakespeare is wonderful, but he used too many clichés." Furthermore, many of them are quoted incorrectly. What a wonderful thing it is to know that "to gild the lily" should be "To gild refined gold, to paint the lily,/To throw a perfume on the violet" (*King John*, Act IV, Scene 2, Lines 11–12). Moreover, many quotes are left incomplete. When someone says, "A little learning is a dangerous thing" (also often misquoted as "a little knowledge"), it might be nice to add, "Drink deep, or taste not the Pierian spring," thus indicating at once your complete knowledge of the quote, and possibly confounding your listener, who may not. This is the type of thing you murmur gently to your companion when someone misquotes the original. It is not suggested that you correct the speaker! A genuinely cultured person merely lets it be known that he or she knows better, but never makes a public correction. It might aptly be misquoted here that "discretion is the better part of culture."

We use so many figures of speech from mythology, legend, and religion that individuals who don't know their sources can be at an actual disadvantage. A recent news report referred to a famous figure as a Nimrod. Could you have correctly identified Nimrod, the mighty hunter, from Genesis X:9? If you couldn't, the rest of the story was unintelligible.

If you happen to be in the house of someone who is not overly generous with his liquid refreshments, you may find there one of those lovely gadgets that hold liquor bottles securely, preventing their removal without a key to the lock. The bottles are always plainly visible, of course. This nasty device is called a tantalus. In Greek Mythology, it was Tantalus's fate to stand in water up to his chin underneath boughs of fruit, both water and fruit receding whenever he attempted to abate thirst or hunger.

It is nuggets of such golden information on which the following quiz will test you. Such gems sprinkled into the conversation, studding it like truffles in a pâté, will create a wonderful impression of knowledge and culture.

As far as more modern literature is concerned, there is a certain reverse snobbery and culture in *not* reading the current best seller. When you are asked about such a book, the most appropriate answer for a real culture seeker would probably be something along the lines of: "Yes, I intend to get around to it as soon as I've finished that wonderful new translation of Lorca's last book." Such bits of culture can be acquired with minimum effort by scanning current book review sections of the better newspapers and noting books the editors recommend that are clearly not on the best-seller lists. One word of warning! This is a dangerous ploy to try in a truly academic group, where you may be asked very specific questions.

In literature, as in all other fields, what is wildly popular will often be considered by the critics as not really cultured. Edgar Guest, possibly the most widely read poet in America at one time, was the subject of raised eyebrows and sneers from the literary cognoscenti. On the other hand, the cognoscenti weren't always that accurate in their appraisals, either. Who, for example, has ever heard of *The Store,* by T. S. Stribling? It was the Pulitzer Prize winner for best novel of 1933.

It is also acceptable, having read a best seller, to decry it. When you do so, there are certain words that lend a delightful style and grace to your criticism. Such expressions as "vaguely sentimental" and "a reprise of his [her] earlier work" are suitable. Just make sure, in the latter case, that the author does have an earlier work.

For popularized paperback best sellers, those of the gaudy covers and lurid descriptions, probably the best comment you can make (as you will probably read one of these once in a while) is: "I really had to see what all the fuss was about—and *that* sold a million copies?" The preceding comment is acceptable except in the presence of authors who have had a "critical success"—meaning a book that has sold fewer than five thousand copies.

Quoting lines of verse makes for wonderful social currency. Memorize as many as you can. If you have trouble with nonrhymed poetry, look hard for something along the lines of Ogden Nash or Dorothy Parker—acceptable light verse that both rhymes and scans. An effective quote from either, provided it is not one of the hackneyed clichés like Parker's comment on girls who wear glasses, is entirely appropriate in the right circumstances. It is much more effective, of course, if you find a little-known quote that conveys the same idea but is by somebody totally different who sounds like Parker or Nash. Take, for example, the couplet: " 'Tis pity wine is so deleterious,/For tea and coffee leave us much more serious." Ogden Nash, your listeners might guess. No— George Gordon, Lord Byron.

The final ploy must surely be making up a quote and attributing it to someone well known. It would be highly desirable, of course, to choose a writer whose works are mostly in a language other than English. You may even have the supreme pleasure of hearing your own witty bon mot (and if it isn't witty, why are you saying it?) quoted back to you on some future occasion. Do try to be careful, of course, not to misquote or misattribute a statement in front of its author.

1. Where were the Greek gods reputed to live?
   a. On the Acropolis in Athens
   b. On Mount Olympus
   c. On an island in the Aegean Sea

2. Name any two of the Seven Wonders of the World (1 point for each and 1 extra credit for more than 4).
   a. Parthenon
   b. Stone Boat of Peking
   c. Cleopatra's Needle
   d. Forum at Rome
   e. Colosseum
   f. London Bridge
   g. Pyramids of Egypt
   h. Gardens of Semiramis at Babylon
   i. Statue of Zeus at Olympia, by Phidias
   j. Temple of Diana (or Artemis) at Ephesus
   k. Mausoleum at Halicarnassus
   l. Colossus at Rhodes
   m. Pharos of Egypt
   n. Walls of Babylon
   o. Palace of Cyprus

3. What are the Sagas?
   a. Norwegian morality plays
   b. A collection of Scandinavian ballads and folk songs
   c. Historical and mythological traditions of Scandinavian and Germanic culture

4. In Scandinavian mythology, what exactly is Valhalla?
   a. A place in Germany, guarded by dragons
   b. A mythical island in the North Sea
   c. The heaven inhabited by slain warriors

5. Who was the owner of Babe, the blue ox?
   a. Paul Bunyan
   b. John Henry
   c. M. Morefill

6. Rabelais was a famous author. His profession was something totally different. What was he?
   a. Courtier
   b. Physician
   c. Painter

7. There was a famous philosopher known as Kung Fu-tse, whose works have passed into literature and philosophy. He is better known under another name. Who was he?
   a. Buddha
   b. Emperor Lung Kai-schwee
   c. Confucius

8. Why are the *Canterbury Tales*, by Chaucer, considered a landmark in English literature?
   a. They are the first stories ever written about real people
   b. They had a plot, whereas previous stories were merely anecdotes
   c. They were written in English on English themes

9. What was the *Book of the Dead* in ancient Egypt?
   a. A memorial to the dead pharaohs
   b. A religious book of prayers for mourners to study
   c. A book of advice and guidance for the dead, with instructions

10. In Muslim tradition, what is Al Borak?
    a. Heaven
    b. The netherworld
    c. The horse that was received into Paradise

11. Which famous operetta in English was patterned on the exploits of the French poet François Villon?
    a. *The Threepenny Opera*
    b. *The Beggars' Opera*
    c. *The Vagabond King*

12. The *Decameron* is described as having been composed by a party of ladies and gentlemen shut up together voluntarily for a considerable period of time. Why had they removed themselves like this?

a. They had all been banished by the king
b. They were escaping the summer heat in Florence
c. They were trying to escape the plague

13. Sir Thomas More's most famous work, *Utopia,* the forerunner of many works about an ideal society, was written in England in 1516. In what language was it written?
a. Latin
b. French
c. English

14. What famous literary character lived at 221B Baker Street in London?
a. David Copperfield
b. Dr. Jekyll
c. Sherlock Holmes

15. What was the "Five-Foot Shelf"?
a. Five feet of French and Latin literature, sold as a set in the eighteenth century
b. The complete works of Shakespeare
c. A collection of 418 works selected by Dr. Eliot of Harvard

16. Which novel by Charles Dickens is assumed to be autobiographical?
a. *Sense and Sensibility*
b. *David Copperfield*
c. *Great Expectations*

17. Why are Gothic novels called Gothic?
   a. Originally written by Germans (Goths)
   b. Published by the publishing firm of M. Gothia and Sons
   c. Describe events occurring in Gothic-style castles

18. A famous character in Sheridan's play *The Rivals* gave her name to amusing misuses of words. Who was she?
   a. Mrs. Spooner
   b. Mrs. Malaprop
   c. Mrs. Euphemism

19. Helen of Troy was responsible, the story claims, for the start of the Trojan War. What did she do?
   a. Refused to marry the king of Troy
   b. Ran away with Ulysses
   c. Was already married and ran away with Paris

20. Between Scylla and Charybdis means between two equally difficult situations. Just what were the original Scylla and Charybdis?
   a. Two sea monsters
   b. A famous mountain with a series of dangerous passes, Scylla and Charybdis
   c. A whirlpool and a rock in a strait

21. Molière, the famous French dramatist, died in a particularly suitable and ironic manner, which has

been commented upon many times. What happened
to him?
   a. Murdered during a murder play
   b. Killed by someone with the same name as one
      of his characters
   c. Died while playing an invalid in his play about
      an invalid

22. What was Dante's most famous work?
   a. *Ballad of Lost Ladies*
   b. *The Rape of the Sabines*
   c. *The Divine Comedy*

23. What is it that makes a sonnet a sonnet?
   a. The subject matter
   b. The twenty-four lines and a-b, a-b rhyme
   c. The fourteen lines with two different sets of
      rhyme schemes

24. What is the best-known work of the Russian author Fyodor Dostoyevsky?
   a. *Crime and Punishment*
   b. *Anna Karenina*
   c. *The Brothers Karamazov*

25. What is the legend traditionally associated with
the Grail?
   a. It belonged to Romulus and Remus
   b. Anyone who drank from it would live forever
   c. It was traditionally the chalice used at the Last
      Supper

26. In Uriah Heep, Dickens created a character who has passed into the language. What was his main characteristic?
    a. Thievery
    b. Honesty
    c. Deceitful humbleness

27. Name two of the chief deities in Egypt at the time of the pharaohs.
    a. Akhenaten
    b. Nefertiti
    c. Isis
    d. Osiris

28. What's a kobold?
    a. A Scandinavian heroine
    b. An Icelandic weapon
    c. A gnome, or house spirit, in German folklore

29. The Grimm brothers collected and apparently wrote many famous fairy tales. This was not their major field, however. In what field were they world-renowned experts?
    a. Painting
    b. Sculpture
    c. Linguistics

30. A particular hotel in New York City was famous for many years because of the literary personages who gathered there, at what was known as the Round Table. What was—and still is—the hotel?

    a. Waldorf-Astoria
    b. Ritz
    c. Algonquin

31. In Stevenson's story *Dr. Jekyll and Mr. Hyde,* which of the characters is the evil alter ego?
    a. Jekyll
    b. Hyde
    c. Neither

32. Who is the hero of Cervantes' great satirical novel, published in 1605 and 1615?
    a. Don Quixote
    b. Milo Filomoro
    c. Don Juan

33. Alexandre Dumas père was famous for his historical novels. They made him one of the most published novelists of the day, and are still read. Pick two of them. Both for full credit.
    a. *The Three Musketeers*
    b. *The Prince and the Pauper*
    c. *The Divine Comedy*
    d. *Twenty Years After*
    e. *The Life of Emile Zola*

34. There was a mythical kingdom where Prince Rupert of Hentzau lived and swashbuckled through such literary and stage adventures as *The Prisoner of Zenda.* What was the name of the kingdom?

a. Transylvania
b. Bosnia-Herzegovina
c. Ruritania

35. Where did Count Dracula live?
    a. In Vienna
    b. In Germany
    c. In Transylvania

36. The anthem played for the President of the United States is "Hail to the Chief." The first line is: "Hail to the chief who in triumph advances." From where do the words come?
    a. "The Battle Hymn of the Republic"
    b. "The Conqueror" march, by John Philip Sousa
    c. "The Lady of the Lake," by Sir Walter Scott

37. From what poem is the well-known line "The Moving Finger writes; and, having writ,/Moves on"?
    a. Shakespeare's Sonnet XXV
    b. Longfellow's "Song of Life"
    c. The *Rubáiyát of Omar Khayyám*

38. Another, often misquoted, saying is "Far from the madding [*not* maddening] crowd." From what does this line come?
    a. The Bible
    b. Shakespeare
    c. Thomas Gray's "Elegy in a Country Churchyard"

39. Another famous quotation is "a woman is only a woman, but a good cigar is a Smoke." Author and poem, please.
    a. Robert W. Service, "Songs of the Yukon"
    b. Mark Twain, "Innocents Abroad"
    c. Rudyard Kipling, "The Betrothed"

40. Which French author put together a collection of fables with morals that rival the collection of Aesop?
    a. Molière
    b. Montesquieu
    c. La Fontaine

41. For the Chinese, which symbol represents lightning, and much of the power of nature?
    a. Waves
    b. Phoenix
    c. Dragon

42. What are the Vedas?
    a. Roman gods
    b. Hindu gods
    c. The sacred books of the Brahmins

43. What are the chief characteristics of the novels of James Joyce, which represent a departure in the form of the novel?
    a. Very short chapters

b. Multiple points of view
c. Stream of consciousness

44. Samuel Pepys wrote a diary of his life in England. In 1665 he wrote about the plague, which had attacked the country. His was a real-life account, but a novel was written about it, which is considered a far better description. What was the novel, and who was the novelist?
   a. Daniel Defoe, *Journal of the Plague Year*
   b. Charles Dickens, *Edwin Drood*
   c. Edwin Smith, *The True Tale of the Gruesome Plague*

45. Why are spiders called arachnids?
   a. Linnaeus, who originally classified species, named them after his wife
   b. It describes the body structure of the spider
   c. Spiders are named for a spinner who defied the Greek gods and was turned into a spider

46. To whom do we owe the character of Father Knickerbocker as a symbol of New York City?
   a. Nathaniel Hawthorne
   b. James Fenimore Cooper
   c. Washington Irving

47. In Japanese literature, there is a poetic form known as the haiku. What is it?
   a. A drama

   b. A long narrative poem
   c. A short poem of seventeen syllables

48. Who were Acton, Ellis, and Currer Bell?
   a. Three famous eighteenth-century actresses
   b. Three characters in one of Charlotte Brontë's
      novels
   c. Anne, Emily, and Charlotte Brontë used these
      as pen names

49. Nathaniel Hawthorne is considered one of
America's greatest writers. What was his basic subject?
   a. Narrative poetry on American history
   b. Plays based exclusively on American themes
   c. Novels based on American themes

50. Longfellow wrote a narrative poem, *Evangeline*,
about the expulsion and wanderings of the Acadians.
From where were they expelled, and where did
many of them eventually settle?
   a. From Maine to Florida
   b. From France to Quebec
   c. From Nova Scotia to Louisiana

TOTAL POSSIBLE CORRECT ANSWERS: 55

YOUR SCORE _____

Art, art, and (art)

There is Art, and there is art. Art with a capital A is what the critics write about, and art is generally popular. This division has undoubtedly existed since John Cro-Magnon stood in front of a bison, painted on the wall of a cave, and said to his wife, "I may not know Art, but I know what I like."

The trick in the culture game is to know the difference and take advantage of all the odds in your favor. You can be sure that if you understand exactly what the artist is trying to paint, the critics will not like it. That is, they won't like it at the present time. The patina of age, or the passage of years, seems to make some art into Art.

If you absolutely do not like what you are looking at, fear not. You are not alone. There is no famous painting in the world that hasn't been unmercifully criticized by the same breed of critic that later acclaimed it as a work of genius.

If you don't understand exactly what you are looking at, there are some steps you can take. "Slightly
obscure" is a meaningful phrase, useful in almost any
situation. Just exactly what it means is usually not
clear, and there is often considerable doubt whether
it is a critical remark or praise, which is exactly what
you want. It is equally applicable to what you like and
what you don't like, as it is possible that you like
something you don't understand. A brief comment
on the ingenious use of color will produce the same
general effect. The real problem in discussing Art
comes when you not only do not understand what
you are looking at, but you really don't like it. In
addition, you are well aware that it is Art, and not art.

If your education in this area has been confined to
wall calendars, don't give up hope. You may still par-
ticipate in this game of "the more obscure the better." Here's how:

First, read this chapter. Then check the answers.
Finally, drop into your conversation a fascinating
piece of information about the famous brothers who
are generally considered to be responsible for the oil
painting techniques now used. That's sufficiently interesting, and sufficiently obscure, to give you some
footing in the Art camp. (See question 9.) You might
also want to do some additional research on the artist
of question 40, who has a lesser-known but perhaps
even more fascinating series of engravings showing
architectural details of famous buildings. He is renowned, and almost in the realm of art, for his views
of Rome; but he is high on the Art scale for the architectural drawings.

The same holds true for many of the more obscure personages mentioned here: some of their works are well known, some are not. It is very useful indeed to do a little research to discover a secondary area in which famous people were gifted. For example, Ingres, the famous painter, wanted to be known as a violinist. Thus the second and often minor talent of a well-known artist is sometimes called *violin d'Ingres,* and tossing this into a discussion about talents great and notable will lend you an air of culture.

It really is not considered very chic to stand before a painting and mutter, "My six-year-old could do better than that," although in some recent tests, there were critics unable to determine which paintings had been done by a chimpanzee and which by a professional painter. You can do much better, in terms of criticism, by using words such as "regressive" or "murky." Both statements say the same thing, both are critical and indicate you don't like the painting, but the difference here is crucial; it is one of style.

The same holds true for the other visual arts, such as architecture. One of us stands almost alone in rejoicing that the old Metropolitan Opera House in New York is gone, to be replaced by the new one in Lincoln Center. Despite its Artistic merit, the old opera house had little musical merit in terms of acoustics, and a scoffer usually can overcome critics with some variation of the Art phrase "Form follows function," thus implying at once that he or she is not only musically literate but in the avant-garde of visual and functional architecture.

That is basically the secret of being cultured, in the terms we have defined it, in Art. You must recognize Art when you see it, but you must also be able to express your own tastes and feelings, especially if you don't happen to like the work of Art being discussed. A knowledge of the vocabulary of Art, as we have indicated in the questions that follow, is extremely important. You do want to know the difference between "art trouvé" and "pop art," don't you? Even if you don't like either one, it is nice to be able to say, "Don't you think that style is slightly passé?" Almost everything can be considered slightly passé, so you won't be risking much by that comment. If it *is* slightly passé, you will have scored some points.

Other forms of the visual arts present their own problems. They, too, can be solved with a judicious phrase or two. If you are touring a house that dates from the Victorian period, for example, and you hate everything in the place, it is safe to remark, "All their inhibitions came out in their furnishings." You have given away nothing about your dislike for today's decorator fad, and have simultaneously shown your knowledge of the psychological world of the Victorians.

Tapestries, small pieces of silverwork, jeweled cups, and items such as crystal come under the same general rubric. If you really like what you are looking at, you might bestow upon it the term "restrained elegance," or "joyous exuberance," depending, of course, upon which it is. Other satisfactory expressions of general use might be "pastiche" for anything that you would ordinarily call a mixed-up mess, and "derivative" for something that looks just like everything else you have been looking at. Don't be afraid of negative criticism. A major reexamination now going on of some of the choicest works of gold, enamel, and jewelry indicates that much of it may have been done by a clever forger; until very recently, even the experts were fooled. That's a nice bit of information to store away if anyone praises any piece you thoroughly detest.

You may, of course, find you really like only what is often dismissed by Art critics as "popular taste." Here is your chance to shine. Brush up on some phrases about the beauty of machine technology, the "stark simplicity" of stainless steel as opposed to sterling, and the "naif" quality of popular art. With the right expression on your slightly amused face, and the right phrases, you can even get away with hanging a popular calendar picture on your wall. "So amusing to have examples of naif art as counterpoint. . . ." This may also be the time to toss out the fact that Van Gogh was totally unappreciated by the Art critics while he was alive, and to indicate that what passes for Art may be fad instead. But don't get carried away. Even self-expression has its limits—there is not much anyone can say in defense of a large family of gnomes on the front lawn.

1. The earliest paintings of which we have any record are from the Cro-Magnon period. Where are these found?

    a. Near East
    b. Italy
    c. Southern France and northern Spain

2. Why do Egyptian paintings look unusual to us
today?
    a. No colors
    b. Nonrepresentational
    c. No perspective as we know it

3. It appears as if the earliest Greek statues were not
made from marble. What were they made from and
why do we think so?
    a. Plaster—pieces of statues found
    b. Wood strips glued together—pieces found
    c. Tree trunks—statues carved within form of
       tree trunk

4. Aside from weathering and deterioration, what is
the major difference between Greek statues as we
see them today and the way the Greeks originally
viewed them?
    a. Greeks always viewed them from a long dis-
       tance
    b. Greeks only allowed to view them through a
       screen
    c. Statues were originally painted bright colors

5. Why is the part of the frieze from the Parthenon
that is now in the British Museum called the Elgin
marbles?
    a. Kept in Elgin Room there

b. Found in Elgin, Greece
c. Brought by Lord Elgin

6. The Romans seem to have invented a building material without which they could not have constructed such large edifices as the Colosseum. What was that building material?
   a. Clay bricks
   b. Steel
   c. Concrete

7. What makes an arch a "Roman" arch?
   a. Height
   b. Width
   c. Keystone locks the arch

8. What is the purpose of a flying buttress, as in a cathedral?
   a. Decorative only
   b. Used to protect precious stained glass
   c. To support the roof

9. Who is/are generally considered to have invented the technique of using oil as a painting base?
   a. Michelangelo
   b. Van Eyck brothers
   c. Rembrandt

10. Which family of Florence is considered to be most responsible for making that city a treasure house of art?
    a. Buonarroti

b. Borgia
c. Medici

11. Which painter became famous chiefly for his portraits of the court of Henry VIII?
    a. M. Fillmore
    b. Constable
    c. Holbein

12. From what famous quarry did most of the marble for Italian artworks come?
    a. Rome
    b. Pisa
    c. Carrara

13. What is plateresque architecture?
    a. Silver-plated altar rails
    b. Developed by Platero
    c. A highly decorated and complex architectural style

14. One of Rembrandt's most famous paintings is called *The Night Watch.* It is a group of men shown in darkness. What was it originally?
    a. A portrait painted over because the woman subject objected
    b. A portrait of a group inside a church, and hence dark
    c. A daytime picture, but it was darkened by peat smoke

15. For what was Capability Brown famous?
    a. Painting
    b. Architecture
    c. Landscape gardening

16. One man, in France, was responsible for rebuilding Notre Dame, for reconstructing the walls of Carcassonne, and for many other such achievements in restoring architecture. Who was he?
    a. Lenôtre
    b. Corbusier
    c. Viollet-le-Duc

17. In 1863, French painters who had been rejected by the official Academy formed a group and put on an exhibition called "Salon des Refusés." An American painter, who became extremely well known, was included in the group. Who was he?
    a. J. M. W. Turner
    b. John Stuart
    c. James McNeill Whistler

18. A particular style and school of painting has the title "Impressionism." From what did the title come?
    a. The "impression" the viewer received
    b. The impression of the paintbrush and the heavy paint on the canvas
    c. A painting called *An Impression* which was in the Refusés show

19. What was the Pre-Raphaelite Brotherhood?
    a. A religious group that built beautiful chapels
    b. A group of monks who painted religious scenes
    c. A group of English painters and craftsmen

20. Which American architect built Taliesin and Taliesin West as models of what architecture should be?
    a. I. M. Pei
    b. Frank Lloyd Wright
    c. Frank Sullivan

21. Who was the inventor of the geodesic dome?
    a. John Roebling
    b. Le Corbusier
    c. Buckminster Fuller

22. What is the basic difference between French and British landscape architecture?
    a. One uses trees instead of shrubs
    b. One does not use flowers
    c. French is formal, English more "natural"

23. What is a genre painting?
    a. A painting in a particular type of oil
    b. A painting done in watercolors
    c. A painting of everyday scenes depicting the life of the time

24. What is gouache?
    a. A type of sculpture

b. Another name for collage
c. Watercolor mixed with water and gum

25. What is unusual about the construction of the Solomon R. Guggenheim Museum in New York City?
    a. It has an "exoskeleton" outside
    b. It is all glass
    c. It basically consists of a ramp on which the art is displayed

26. What is the outstanding architectural feature of the Georges Pompidou Center in Paris?
    a. It has a spiral ramp inside for display
    b. It has the supporting structure on the outside
    c. It has no individual exhibit halls

27. Who was the architect of St. Peter's Cathedral in Rome?
    a. Leonardo da Vinci
    b. Giovanni Bernini
    c. Andrea Palladio

28. Which British architect is responsible for dozens of churches in London, as well as Saint Paul's Cathedral?
    a. Grinling Gibbons
    b. Benjamin West
    c. Sir Christopher Wren

29. What is the tallest structure in Washington, D.C.?

    a. The Lincoln Memorial
    b. The Washington Monument
    c. The Kennedy Center

30. What famous American painter specialized in scenes of small-town American life?
    a. Norman Rockwell
    b. Gluyas Williams
    c. William Remington

31. What is the name, in French or Italian, of the painting we know as the Mona Lisa?
    a. La Dame Liese or La Donna Liesa
    b. La Gioconda or La Belle Gioconde
    c. La Dame qui rit

32. Who was the original illustrator of many of Dickens's works, whose etchings became famous on this account?
    a. Thomas Rowlandson
    b. George Cruikshank
    c. William Hogarth

33. Which architect designed Washington, D.C.?
    a. Sir Christopher Wren
    b. Pierre L'Enfant
    c. Baron Haussman

34. Rembrandt is known very largely for his paintings. He was also highly skilled in another field of art. What was it?

a. Sculpture
b. Architecture
c. Engraving

35. Auguste Rodin is usually considered to be the most important nineteenth-century exponent of his métier. What was it?
    a. Engraving
    b. Watercolor
    c. Sculpture

36. The painting *Nude Descending a Staircase* caused a furor when it was first exhibited. Who painted it?
    a. Picasso
    b. Matisse
    c. Duchamp

37. Who was the sculptor who created the Statue of Liberty?
    a. Augustus Saint-Gaudens
    b. Mrs. Peter Scott
    c. Frédéric A. Bartholdi

38. What is generally considered to be the oldest map known?
    a. Mercator's *mappa mundi*
    b. Columbus's map drawn upon his return from his first voyage, in 1493
    c. A Babylonian clay tablet

39. Who is credited with the first drawings of maps showing the earth and distances in proportion, allowing for curvature?
    a. Columbus
    b. Mercator
    c. Hakluyt

40. There is a famous set of views of Rome, done in a romanticized style and showing antique ruins. Who was the engraver?
    a. Canaletto
    b. Ruskin
    c. Piranesi

41. A famous edition of the Bible was illustrated by a noted engraver. Who was he?
    a. Rembrandt
    b. Doré
    c. Cruickshank

42. An English painter became famous (initially infamous) by painting light, storms, wind, and similar nonvisible phenomena. Who was he?
    a. Turner
    b. Whistler
    c. Gainsborough

43. A painter of the Middle Ages specialized in demons, devils, and fantastic allegorical scenes, including some imaginative and unusual tortures. Who was he?

    a. Bosch
    b. Brueghel
    c. Dürer

44. What is the only man-made structure that could be seen from the moon?
    a. World Trade Center
    b. Hoover Dam
    c. Great Wall of China

45. What was the original purpose of the Taj Mahal?
    a. Art gallery
    b. Reception hall
    c. Mausoleum

46. There is an art form consisting of layers of paper or other such material glued or attached to a background. What is it called?
    a. Decoupage
    b. Pastel
    c. Collage

47. There is a school of art that consists of presenting real objects (not painted) for display as artworks. What is this usually called?
    a. Dadaism
    b. Cubism
    c. Objets trouvés

48. Fairly recently, a school of art has developed that consists of superrealistic portrayals of such things as

soup cans, movie posters, advertisements, and the
like. What is this called?
    a. Surrealism
    b. Art Nouveau
    c. Pop art

49. Who is the Spanish architect noted for his cathedral and other unusual buildings in Barcelona?
    a. San Pellegrino
    b. Milagroso Filamoria
    c. Antonio Gaudí

50. For what art is the pueblo of San Ildefonso in
New Mexico particularly noted?
    a. Stone carvings
    b. Wall paintings
    c. Pottery

51. For what is the Gobelins famous?
    a. Crystal
    b. Paintings
    c. Tapestries

52. There is a chateau in France that is built over a
river, on arches, and is so unusual in appearance that
it is frequently shown on posters and in travel broc-
hures. Which chateau is it?
    a. Chambord
    b. Versailles
    c. Chenonceaux

53. Where is the Hall of Mirrors?
    a. Buckingham Palace, London
    b. Schönbrunn Palace, Vienna
    c. Versailles, France

54. In what museum is the *Winged Victory?*
    a. British Museum
    b. National Museum of Athens
    c. Louvre

55. Which museum has a full-size Egyptian temple built within its walls?
    a. Metropolitan Museum of Art, New York
    b. National Museum of Egypt, Cairo
    c. Louvre, Paris

TOTAL POSSIBLE SCORE: 55

YOUR SCORE _____

Airs and Affectations: Etiquette and Manners

Our meals, our manners, and what we call our mores are so basic a part of our lives that they are often ignored when culture is considered. George Bernard Shaw, a wise and witty observer of life, recorded some of this in *Pygmalion*. No one is born knowing which fork to use, or which wine goes with game, nor even whether "I" or "me" is correct in a given context. Yet judgment can be passed on an individual in these areas as firmly as it can be in the more typically cultured fields of art, music, and literature. Subconscious judgments are made by all of us, all the time, on the basis of likes or dislikes in food and drink. Not so subconscious judgments are made on the basis of visible manners. Thus the truly cultured must be vigilant.

The world is basically divided into two categories:

those who eat snails, and those who consider them garden pests. The same could be said for aficionados of frogs' legs, sour cream, and even marshmallows. There are those who are firmly convinced that the law declaring marshmallows fit for human consumption was repealed years ago; and those who still consider them not only desirable but luxurious ingredients in such food items as gelatin salads and baked sweet potato casseroles. Today, there is also a wide gap between the "meat and potatoes" crowd and those who are following "nouvelle cuisine" along the kiwi-fruit-and-rare-duck-breast road.

Manners pose many considerations. Here, too, upbringing and geographical location may determine culture. We are speaking of manners in terms of the arbiters of such things: the authors of books of etiquette. Some knowledge of what is contained therein could be considered a requisite for culture, even if the cultured person chooses not to follow the rules slavishly.

Naturally, someone who flouts the rules should do so with a smile, and with a comment that indicates he or she is fully aware of the rules but is on a level high enough to ignore them. "So amusing" should, of course, be said in a self-congratulatory manner when you are the one doing the rule-breaking. On the other hand, if you are in a situation where someone else is being iconoclastic, the same "So amusing," with the appropriate inflection, can be a devastating comment without being actually rude. The cultured

person is never *obviously* rude, unless he or she is
world-famous. In that case, rudeness can be considered witty. Until you reach the status of a Monte
Python or a Joan Rivers, it is probably safer not to try
this particular technique.

As far as mores are concerned, there is a psychological truism that says a fact is anything you learned
before you were four years old. Whether you eat
dinner or supper in the evening is a matter of mores
learned at your mother's knee. The mores, or social
customs and beliefs, of a group may not be set in
concrete, but they are just as firmly embedded in our
lives. What we often don't realize is that they are
merely that—mores and not laws. American mores,
for example, say that lamb should be cooked until
well done. Even new cookbooks give temperatures
that produce well-done lamb, and an attempt to ob-
tain rare lamb in an American restaurant occasionally produces the same effect as asking the chef to
serve poison. In France, on the other hand, lamb is
usually pink if not red. So much for cultural dictates.

It is the responsibility of anyone who wishes to be
considered cultured to be aware of mores, examine
them, and decide whether or not to utilize them in
a particular situation. A friend of ours, an American,
who had never been abroad before, bought himself
freedom across a closed border in a country where he
had been trapped by a war. (He did it by offering the
border guard who came to examine his papers a pack
of cigarettes. In the pack was a ten-dollar bill rolled
up to replace a cigarette, and he made sure the guard

could see it. The guard took a cigarette, then the
pack, and the border opened for him—but not for
others.) Our friend had seen this ploy shortly before
in a spy movie, and being both cultured and clever,
had filed it away as an alternative to his usual behav-
ior.

A cultured person adapts to the surrounding
mores. It isn't going to do you much good not to, like
demanding dinner at 6 P.M. in Spain. The cultured
person blends into the surroundings in manner, but
stands out in style. This means that while a cowboy
hat and jeans may not be the standard dress in London, if you really are a cowboy they are entirely
acceptable, except for a presentation at Buckingham
Palace. After all, the Roosevelts entertained the king
and queen of England with a "weenie roast" during
their visit to this country. Royalty obviously enjoyed
it and adapted to local mores.

In this area, as in the others we discuss, there are
strategies to help you when your manners have failed
you. Should someone offer a correction (which would
be altogether uncultured of them), announce,
"That's very enlightening." The remark is applicable
to almost any occasion. It has the further advantage
of not meaning anything much but sounding pro-
found.

Some of the more recondite facts contained in our
quiz will be of great assistance in your accultura-
tional process. Especially in the area of food and
wine, conversation about the food and the wine is
often as important as their ingestion. A quiet com-

ment, when at a wine tasting, regretting that you
have never tasted a pre-phylloxera wine will establish your bona fides. It can be useful, for example, to
compare a new, popular cookbook with one of the
earliest and least known, a name you will find in the
quiz that follows.

Don't disdain stopping by the local gourmet shop
for a quick, self-taught course in whatever is new in
the vegetable line. That could save you from discard-
ing, with a grimace, the red-edged lettuce that you
would otherwise be sure was wilted.

The last word or words on the subject were said
many years ago. Pick the quotation you prefer: *O
tempora, O mores! Autres temps, autres moeurs.*
They express both dismay and resignation, the
proper set of attitudes with which to regard the
whole subject.

1. Most cookbook collectors are familiar with the
very earliest collection of articles concerned chiefly
with cooking and eating. Dated 230 A.D., it is considered a landmark in this type of writing. Who is the
author, or what is the book?
   a. *Deipnosophists*
   b. *De Gustibus*
   c. *Satyricon*

2. What is the earliest actual cookbook, with recipes,
of which we have any record?
   a. Mrs. Beeton's

b. Coelius Apicius' *De Re Culinaria*
c. Escoffier's

3. Many ancient Roman recipes called for a sauce called *garum*. What is it?
   a. Wine vinegar
   b. Pickled, preserved olives
   c. A sauce made from fermented fish

4. Some French wines advertise themselves as Premier Grand Cru, Grand Cru, etc. On what do they base this classification?
   a. Their own opinion, based on sales
   b. Regional councils
   c. A government classification of 1855

5. What is generally considered to be the finest wine of the Médoc, in Bordeaux, the crème de la crème— or the vin du vin, to be specific?
   a. A collection of four: Château Lafite, Château Margaux, Château Latour, and Château Haut-Brion
   b. Château Lafite-Rothschild
   c. There is none, because all were of the same quality

6. What is considered beyond question to be the finest sweet white Bordeaux wine?
   a. Trockenbeerenauslese
   b. Madeira
   c. Château d'Yquem

7. From whom, what, or where did sherry get its name?
    a. Sir James Sherry, its inventor
    b. Jerez de la Frontera, in Spain
    c. The sherry grapes used in making it

8. Wheat, when used for bread, enables people to do without meat or fish. The same is not true for potatoes. Why?
    a. Wheat has more nitrogenous material
    b. It is more filling
    c. Potatoes lack vitamin C

9. What was apparently the first fermented beverage?
    a. Beer
    b. Mead
    c. Wine

10. What are some of the vegetables introduced from the New World to Europe?
    a. String beans, eggplant, turnips
    b. Lettuce and spinach
    c. Potatoes, tomatoes, and various "hot" peppers

11. What is a Salisbury steak, which appears on many menus, and why is it so called?
    a. A cut developed in Salisbury, England
    b. A chopped meat patty prescribed by Dr. Salisbury for easy digestion
    c. A steak with "Salisbury" sauce on it

12. What is the difference, at the table, between French service and Russian service?
   a. French is more elegant
   b. French is the setting of full platters on the table before guests sit down; Russian involves serving one guest at a time
   c. French is multicourse; Russian is one or two courses only

13. What major disaster in the vineyards of Europe changed the character and type of wines over the last hundred years?
   a. Floods in 1880, which washed away centuries-old vines
   b. The phylloxera louse, which ruined the root-stocks
   c. Ten years of freezing winter weather, which altered the character of the vines that could survive

14. An aperitif called Pineau des Charentes is becoming popular. What is it?
   a. A light, nonalcoholic fizzy drink
   b. A new wine, developed within the last few years from a hybrid planting
   c. A wine in which the fermentation has been stopped by the addition of Cognac

15. Most German wines of any consequence are of one color only. Which one?
   a. Red

b. White

c. Rosé

16. What is a varietal wine?
    a. Any wine named for the location where it is grown
    b. Any wine named for its major grape
    c. A wine named for the chateau that processed it

17. Which is the dryest (least sweet) champagne?
    a. Brut
    b. Dry
    c. Extra Dry

18. Where and when did the first real restaurants appear?
    a. In France in 1500, as part of the mail routes
    b. In England, with the famous taverns
    c. In France, just before the French revolution

19. Which United States President was noted for his fine table, his chef, and his custom of growing his own vegetables?
    a. John F. Kennedy
    b. Thomas Jefferson
    c. Abraham Lincoln

20. What is the possibly apocryphal story about Parmentier and his attempts to popularize the potato in France?

a. It was served with brand-new recipes, invented by Parmentier
b. He made the army serve it to the soldiers, who loved French-fried potatoes
c. He guarded the potato fields carefully but with the intent of having the plants stolen, and thus made them desirable

21. Who is often credited with introducing not only fine cuisine, but also the fork, into France?
a. Rabelais
b. Henry IV
c. Catherine de' Medici

22. Who is popularly, but probably not accurately, credited with introducing spaghetti to Italy?
a. Columbus
b. Lorenzo the Magnificent
c. Marco Polo

23. What is haggis?
a. Hearts, lungs, and livers of a sheep or lamb made into a pudding, cooked in a sheep's stomach
b. Porridge flavored with Scottish whisky and cooked in sausage casing
c. A malt brew added to a vegetable stew

24. What seems to be the derivation of "chop suey" as applied to Chinese food?
a. Cantonese dialect for "food eaten with chopsticks"

b. A phonetic rendering of Chinese words meaning "assorted things"
c. Chinese for "stir-fried vegetables and noo-
   dles"

25. What is the national dish of many North African
countries, or at least the dish most often served?
   a. Rice and lamb
   b. Couscous
   c. Baba ganouj

26. What is the distinguishing characteristic of
such meats as Bundnerfleisch, Parma ham, and carpaccio?
   a. Thin slicing
   b. All are pork of some variety
   c. The meats are raw

27. For what was Columbus searching, in his voyage
to the Indies?
   a. China
   b. The so-called Spice Islands
   c. A route around the world

28. A good eater is sometimes described as a good
trencherman. What does this mean?
   a. Someone strong enough to dig trenches
   b. A trencher was originally the plate, consisting
      of bread, which was also eaten

c. A combined knife and fork combination was called a trencher, since it dug trenches in the food

29. Au gratin is usually assumed to mean with cheese, but cheese is not really the essential. What does au gratin really mean?
    a. Baked in the oven
    b. With a crust on it
    c. Baked spaghetti

30. Who is popularly credited with the invention of champagne?
    a. Marie Antoinette
    b. Louis XIV
    c. Dom Perignon

31. What is the difference between those two widely discussed phenomena "nouvelle cuisine" and "cuisine minceur"?
    a. The first is French, the second Italian
    b. One is marked by unusual combinations, the second by diet principles
    c. There is no basic difference

32. Esau sold his brithright for a mess of pottage. What was the actual food?
    a. Lentil soup or stew
    b. Beef broth
    c. Cheese

33. What is the common name in Europe for what we call corn, or sweet corn?
   a. Rye
   b. Maize
   c. Wheat

34. In British books, the name "hock" will often be found, referring to a type of wine. What kind is it, and what do we call it?
   a. French white, called Graves
   b. German white, called Sylvaner
   c. German Rhine wine

35. What kind or type of wines are Spumanti, Sekt, and Mousseux?
   a. Red wines
   b. Expensive rosé wines
   c. Sparkling wines

36. Besides the grape, what is the essential ingredient in producing the naturally sweet wines of Sauternes, the Trockenbeerenauslese of Germany, etc.?
   a. A good deal of added sugar
   b. A type of mold called *Botrytis cinerea*
   c. A small amount of brandy

37. What is the difference between Sauterne wine and Sauternes wine?
   a. None

b. One is American, the other French; otherwise none

c. Sauternes is French sweet wine; Sauterne can be almost any white wine

38. From what crustacean do "lobster tails" come?
    a. Small American lobsters
    b. Very large shrimp
    c. Spiny lobsters something like crayfish

39. What is the proper technique for a Scandinavian *skål* or *skoal?*
    a. A man catches the eye of another and toasts, including the host but not the hostess
    b. Everybody toasts everybody else
    c. No rules

40. In what order do men and women walk behind the headwaiter in a fine restaurant?
    a. Different rules, depending upon circumstances, but usually women behind the headwaiter
    b. The headwaiter should not show you to your table, only the maître d'hôtel
    c. In the most convenient order

41. What is the difference between European Plan and American Plan at a hotel?
    a. European Plan means tips included
    b. American Plan means your menu is à la carte in contrast to a fixed meal

    c. American Plan means with meals, European
       Plan means without meals

42. What is the correct order for taking food from a
smorgasbord table?
    a. Take whatever you like
    b. Hot foods first, then return for the cold dishes
       and the salads
    c. Fish first, then salads, then hot foods

43. What is the usual reason for decanting a wine?
    a. To leave behind the sediment at the bottom of
       the bottle
    b. To facilitate serving
    c. To avoid bottle leaks on the tablecloth

44. According to the etiquette books (but not, often,
general practice), what is the only time a woman
should use her first name, last name, and the title
Mrs.?
    a. Signing a personal letter
    b. Writing a business letter
    c. As a divorced woman

45. What is the appropriate tip for the purser on a
ship, if he has been extremely helpful?
    a. Ten percent of the fare
    b. Three percent of the fare to the purser, seven
       percent to everyone else
    c. The purser is a ship's officer, and is never
       tipped

46. Which shape glass is preferred for serving champagne?
    a. The champagne saucer with a hollow stem
    b. A "flute"
    c. Any wineglass for white wine

47. Which is considered more correct to serve before dinner, a cream sherry, or a fino or Amontillado sherry?
    a. A dry sherry like a fino or Amontillado
    b. A sweet sherry like a cream (Bristol Cream, for example)
    c. Sherry is an after-dinner wine

48. What is the general rule to follow if you are serving several wines with dinner?
    a. No special rules
    b. The wine appropriate to the food, regardless of type
    c. White before red, light before heavy, generally

49. In what order should utensils be placed at a place setting?
    a. All forks on the left, knives and spoons on the right
    b. From the outside in; one uses the ones farthest from the plate first
    c. Inside out; one uses the ones closest to the plate first

50. What is the correct form to use in congratulating
the bride at her wedding?
    a. "Congratulations and best wishes"
    b. Anything you want to say
    c. The bride should only be wished happiness or
       something similar

51. What are the obligations incurred when you re-
ceive a wedding announcement?
    a. None
    b. A present
    c. A personal reply

52. Who gives the bridal shower or showers?
    a. Her mother and closest female relatives
    b. No special rule
    c. No family members

53. What are the duties of a best man at a wedding?
    a. To safeguard the ring
    b. To act as a witness
    c. Everything he can do for the groom

54. Is it correct to eat asparagus with the fingers? Or
lamb chops? Or corn on the cob?
    a. Yes, at home
    b. No, never
    c. Depending on circumstances, yes for all of
       them

55. Who steps into a revolving door first, the lady or
the gentleman?
   a. Common sense about what is easiest
   b. Man
   c. Lady

TOTAL POSSIBLE SCORE: 55

YOUR SCORE _____

Art in the Dark: Music, Theater, Dance, and Film

This is one area the true cognoscente needs to know thoroughly. Even in deserted Western mining towns there are magnificent deserted opera houses, for first came the gold, second came the wives, and third came the strivings for culture. In the past, a box at the opera, almost anywhere, conferred social status and cachet upon its possessors, and opera attendees (those in the boxes, at least) were listed in the social news. With such a history of snob appeal, the performing arts are *must* learning.

On the other hand, folk dancing has now become just as popular among the cultured as opera has always been. It is possible, then, to put your liking for many popular performances in the mainstream. After all, theater, ballet, concerts, and dance all began as popular amusements. The Greek theaters were large enough to hold everybody in town—no "scalpers" there. And no nonsense about only the upper classes going to hear the latest play. Any good student of Shakespeare knows that some of the more obscure allusions are actually extremely earthy jokes, done in the popular jargon of the day, and obviously aimed at the man in the street, who that night was on a bench of the Globe Theater.

It is thus possible to place yourself on record as liking almost any of the performing arts without doing yourself any damage. You can learnedly discuss the rise of the theater from its popular beginnings, dragging in the miracle plays en route, and their descendant of today in Salzburg. Point out the derivation of the ballet, via those peasant dances, and contrive to give the impression that liking the performing arts is both democratic and cultured at the same time. You might also want to get in a few discreet jibes at the failure of critics to recognize the worth of much popular work, and especially the exclusion of large numbers of the public, mostly on financial grounds, from performances. A brief mention of Wagner's troubles in staging his operas, an even briefer mention of Verdi's initial failures, and you have established yourself as both a connoisseur of the performing arts and a champion of the general public.

You might, however, refuse to admit that anyone since Tchaikovsky or Rachmaninoff has had anything to say in the musical line. There is an easy and effective way to handle that. Simply turn the previous argument on its head. (Only a poor argument won't work in both directions.) Point out that only the classics are truly worthy. Point out that the critics who failed to admire these magnificent artists now praise them highly, but so does the general public. You can afford to express your strong preference for those tried and true pieces which have stood the test of time and still draw overflow crowds whenever they are performed.

This ploy, to be really successful, requires a fair amount of name dropping of highly praised composers or playwrights whose works have not stood up well over the last fifty years. There are a good many of them, so that it should not be difficult for you, with a minimum of research, to have some effective ammunition.

It is also possible to present both positions, and more, as long as you don't do it at the same party. You can be the defender of the popular taste, the defender of the classics, and the staunch champion of the avant garde—depending upon the appropriate circumstances—if you keep one fact firmly in mind: The well-known critics are your target. If they like some performance very much right now, say you want to wait and see what the judgment of time will be. If they don't like it because it is too popular, explain that you trust the popular judgment. If they simply dislike it altogether, reply that you don't trust their recognition of what is good and what is not, as demonstrated by the failures of critical judgment in the past.

There are a few caveats here, naturally. Engaging

in this sort of one-upmanship means you had better brush up on your facts. The questions in this chapter should prepare you for any difficult moments in your culture hopping. You must also be prepared to deal with the individual who will try the most unacceptable tactic of trying to get one up on you. If someone brings up a name, or a work, with which you are unfamiliar, simply remark, "Of course, if you consider . . . appropriate to this discussion, I can't go any further." Please observe that you have told the exact and literal truth—you can't go any further. You may, on the other hand, find some rather obscure facts with which to dazzle your listeners. If you can't bring a little-known person, or play, or opera into a discussion to show up all these would-be snobs, what good is this book? We have procured, from reliable sources, enough of such ammunition to give you a steady supply of salvos in any such contest.

1. What is the derivation of the word "tragedy," as applied to the stage?
   a. From the name of the Greek god of tragedy
   b. Ode to the *tragos,* or goat, which personified Dionysus, god of wine and revelry
   c. From the location of the first Greek theater

2. Why do we have no records of famous actresses in the time of Henry VIII or Queen Elizabeth I?
   a. Actresses were not allowed on the stage
   b. The records were all destroyed in the great fire of London

    c. Queen Elizabeth was jealous and would not
       allow it

3. Who is generally given the credit for inventing
"perspective views" on the stage, as scenery?
    a. Shakespeare
    b. Bernini
    c. Palladio

4. What is "plainsong"?
    a. Nonpolyphonic unison vocal chant
    b. Song without instrumental accompaniment
    c. All one note

5. Who developed the system of musical notation
which meant that once music was written, it would
always be performed in basically the same form?
    a. Bach
    b. Guido of Arezzo
    c. M. de Filmaure

6. What is the oldest tune of which we have any
record?
    a. "Ave Maria"
    b. "The Farmer in the Dell"
    c. Tune now called "He's a Jolly Good Fellow"

7. As far as can be told from the records, where was
the first official performance of what was called ballet?
    a. At the court of the Medicis in Italy

b. At the court of Henry VIII in England
c. Paris in 1581

8. Who wrote the *Saint John Passion,* the *Saint Matthew Passion,* and *Art of the Fugue?*
   a. Handel
   b. Bach
   c. Lully

9. Who composed the former Austrian national anthem, which also appears in the "Kaiser" quartet?
   a. Mozart
   b. Wagner
   c. Haydn

10. As far as the records show, who wrote the first opera in German?
    a. Wagner
    b. Mozart
    c. J. S. Bach

11. What was the instrument that Bach and Mozart used instead of today's piano?
    a. Pianoforte
    b. Harpsichord
    c. Organ

12. Who was the singer called the "Swedish Nightingale"?
    a. Jenny Lind

b. Lillie Langtry
c. Kirsten Flagstad

13. What operas comprise the series *Der Ring des Nibelungen* by Richard Wagner?
a. *The Waterfall of Valhalla, Sieglinde*
b. *The Flying Nibelung* and *The Dutchman's Ring*
c. *Das Rheingold, Die Walküre, Siegfried, Die Götterdämmerung*

14. What is *opéra bouffe?*
a. Serious opera
b. Opera with ballet
c. Comic opera

15. What are the distinguishing characteristics of a ballad?
a. It is always sung by a woman
b. Every other line rhymes
c. It is a popular narrative song with refrain

16. Give a description of the form of a sonata.
a. Composition for one or two instruments, written in three or four movements
b. A composition for orchestra, with two movements
c. Composition for violin only

17. Sarah Kemble Siddons, one of the first of the famous British actresses, was so well thought of that

she has a statue in Westminster Abbey. What was her most renowned role?

   a. Ophelia

   b. Juliet

   c. Lady Macbeth

18. A comedy is often called a farce. What is the derivation of this term?

   a. The humor is "forced"

   b. It was usually an interlude "stuffed" (French *farcie*) into a play

   c. It is the French spelling for the word meaning "funny"

19. What were two of the best-known works of Sophocles, the Greek playwright?

   a. The *Odyssey* and the *Iliad*

   b. *The Women* and *The Furies*

   c. *Oedipus Tyrannus* (or *Rex*) and *Antigone*

20. For what was Isadora Duncan famous?

   a. Opera singing

   b. Painting

   c. Dancing

21. What is the unusual feature of Gustav Mahler's Eighth Symphony?

   a. It does not exist

   b. It is called a symphony but is actually not in symphony form

   c. It requires a thousand performers

22. What is the most famous American stage family —including two brothers and a sister—of the early to middle twentieth century?

    a. The Bernhardts

    b. The Lunts

    c. The Barrymores

23. King Ludwig of Bavaria had a special theater constructed in which he had Wagnerian opera performed. What was unusual about the performances?

    a. They were only acted, not sung

    b. The king himself performed

    c. They were performed for an audience of one —the king

24. The actor Edmund Kean portrayed one of Shakespeare's characters in a way that has been called the touchstone against which other performances were measured. What was this role?

    a. Hamlet

    b. Puck

    c. Shylock

25. The Tony Awards for theatrical excellence in several categories are given annually. For what or whom are they named?

    a. Anthony Adverse

    b. Tony M. Fillmoeurs

    c. Antoinette Perry

26. Emmy Awards are given every year for outstanding performances in many areas of television.
For what or whom are they named?
    a. Emma Willard
    b. Emma Hamilton
    c. The name is made up

27. *The Birth of a Nation,* produced in 1915, was a
landmark in the history of the motion picture, because of its story, advanced technique, and style.
Who is credited with this movie?
    a. David Wark Griffith
    b. Charlie Chaplin
    c. Frank Capra

28. Sir Arthur Sullivan and Sir William S. Gilbert
wrote the Gilbert and Sullivan operettas. Who wrote
the words and who wrote the music?
    a. Gilbert wrote the words and Sullivan wrote
       the music
    b. Gilbert wrote the music, Sullivan the words
    c. Sullivan wrote the music and the words, Gil-
       bert staged the plays

29. Who wrote the American song "The Battle
Hymn of the Republic"?
    a. Julia Ward Howe
    b. Stephen Foster
    c. Thomas More

30. Who is probably the most famous Norwegian composer?
    a. Edvard Munch
    b. Edvard Grieg
    c. Franz Kafka

31. An American playwright well known for musical comedies earlier wrote such plays as *Merton of the Movies* and *The Royal Family*. Who was he?
    a. George S. Kaufman
    b. Tennessee Williams
    c. Moss Hart

32. Who was Feodor Ivanovich Chaliapin (aside from being a Russian)?
    a. A world chess champion
    b. A famous basso
    c. A Russian Nobel Prize winner in Literature

33. Who were the original troubadors?
    a. Singers who appeared during the intermissions of French plays
    b. Church composers
    c. French minstrels of the eleventh to thirteenth centuries

34. Who wrote the operetta *The Merry Widow?*
    a. Franz Lehár
    b. Johann Strauss
    c. Rudolf of Millard

35. In the old Italian comedies, and in pantomines, who is the sweetheart of Columbine?
   a. Columbus
   b. Colette
   c. Harlequin

36. What is the name of the theater in Paris that has given its name to horror shows in general?
   a. Madame Tussaud's
   b. Paris Opera
   c. Grand Guignol

37. What is the theme of Wagner's opera *The Flying Dutchman?*
   a. A mutiny against a captain by his crew
   b. A disguised story of Icarus
   c. A captain condemned to sail forever because of his impiety

38. Who was known as the "Jazz Singer"?
   a. Eddie Cantor
   b. Fats Waller
   c. Al Jolson

39. In what city in the United States is jazz supposed to have originated?
   a. New Orleans
   b. Memphis
   c. New York

40. Who was the most famous Russian dancer of the early part of the twentieth century?
   a. Boris Godunov
   b. Vaslav Nijinsky
   c. I. Stravinsky

41. Karel Čapek wrote a play whose title gave us a word in common use today. What was the play and the word?
   a. *Armageddon*
   b. *R.U.R.* (last *R* is for Robot)
   c. *Video*

42. What is generally considered the earliest true opera?
   a. *Dafne*
   b. *Carmen*
   c. *Aïda*

43. Eugene O'Neill, the American dramatist, won several Pulitzer Prizes. For what type of drama was he noted?
   a. Humor
   b. Musical comedies
   c. Tragedies—all but one

44. What was Kurt Weill's claim to fame?
   a. Famous actor
   b. Famous dancer
   c. Composer of operas

45. During the 1930s a great many children in the United States had their first contact with classical music through radio programs specifically designed for schoolchildren and presented during school hours. Who developed and produced these?
    a. John Philip Sousa
    b. Herbert M. Hoover
    c. Walter Damrosch

46. During what war was "The Star Spangled Banner," our national anthem, written?
    a. American Revolution
    b. War of 1812
    c. The Civil War (The War Between the States)

47. A famous pianist, composer and interpreter of the works of Schumann, Liszt, and Rubinstein, among others, was also elected premier of his country. Who was it?
    a. Frédéric Chopin
    b. Jean Sibelius
    c. Ignace Paderewski

48. Who was, and is, generally considered the greatest Wagnerian soprano of this century?
    a. Jenny Lind
    b. Maria Jeritza
    c. Kirsten Flagstad

49. What were the "miracle plays" of the Middle Ages?

a. Enactments of the Nativity
b. Presentations of Biblical miracles
c. Representations of Bible scenes performed in the church at services

50. Where are the opera houses of La Scala and Covent Garden?
    a. Paris and Berlin
    b. Rome and London
    c. Milan and London

51. When did women first appear on the English stage?
    a. Seventeenth century
    b. Eighteenth century
    c. Twentieth century

52. Sarah Bernhardt is considered to have been one of the greatest actresses of all time. She appeared in one highly improbable role, in which she made an enormous success, when she was close to sixty. What was it?
    a. Camille
    b. Juliet
    c. L'Aiglon, the young son of Napoleon

53. "Die Lorelei" is one of the best-known songs of the Western world. Who wrote the words?
    a. Schiller
    b. Wagner
    c. Heine

54. The contemporary "theater in the round" is actually an adaptation of an earlier form. What?
   a. The ancient Greek theater
   b. Traveling magic shows
   c. Shakespeare's Globe Theater

55. For what was Constantin Stanislavski noted in the world of acting?
   a. The use of inner interpretations of the role
   b. His portrayal of women on the stage
   c. His roles in classical tragedy

TOTAL POSSIBLE SCORE: 55

YOUR SCORE _____

Mastering the Highest Cultural Patter: Math and Science

No one, according to C. P. Snow, can be considered cultured who does not know the second law of thermodynamics. Indeed, if you are not technologically or scientifically cultured, there is a large gap in your awareness. This quiz will also test your knowledge of the first law of thermodynamics, just to make sure that you are doubly cultured. And in case the question arises, there are further laws of thermodynamics, which we do not explain because any aspect of culture can carried past the point of no return. (These laws are known to irreverent students as: You can't win; You can't even break even; and You can't even get out of the game.)

We also include medicine and areas of science dealing with nonabstract principles and discoveries. Surely a cultured person should know just what CAT stands for, even without the foggiest idea of how it works. For many of us, electricity works by flipping a switch, but it is essential to know the words involved in a technical discussion. You can't hope to compete with the experts in their own field, but you should be able to follow a conversation about bits, bytes, RAMs and ROMs. There is almost nothing worse than feeling like an illiterate when those about you are chattering with abandon.

Some sciences, however, we have completely avoided. You will note that there is very little here about illness or psychoanalysis. We defend this to the depths of our inhibited psyches, certain that discussions of illness, or of conversations with one's analyst, hardly come under the heading of culture. Culture is knowing what not to say, as well as knowing what to say. *Mens sana in corpore sano.*

Moreover, we have made no attempt to teach you anything about math. Instead we have presented discoveries by mathematicians that have changed our lives. Unfortunately, these discoveries have not yet included a self-balancing checkbook. Even those who appreciate numbers only when they are on the positive side of the ledger can be edified by stories of the great mathematicians and their findings. A judicious anecdote or two about such a discovery or about a famous mathematician can save you from some of the scorn the mathematically inclined heap upon the mathematically uninclined.

Those individuals who find deep joy and satisfaction in numbers must notice at times that other people do not. Our judicious selection of facts, anecdotes, and bits of light information can help you win more social approval than standing in a group of friends and repeating the binomial theorem, a habit that does a good deal to inhibit subsequent conversation. How much better to drop into the conversational whirlpool the fact that 1983 marked the two hundredth anniversary of the development of manned balloon flight, or the term given to such a phenomenon as the rising and falling sound of a siren or train as it approaches and recedes. It is highly satisfying to be able to drop the name of this effect, and a brief explanation, just as such a noise rises and falls outside.

Of course, for every reaction (favorable), there is an equal and opposite reaction (unfavorable). That is to say, you may want to be above such mundane areas as science and mathematics, and can therefore do as Oxford students did, and call chemistry "Stinks." One Scottish university calls physics by the old term "Natural Philosophy." As one of their graduates explained, the department had been established before physics was developed, and the university saw no reason to change the name of the department just to accommodate a relative newcomer. If you choose to adopt the same tactic, indicate that you feel areas these quizzes cover are suitable for technicians, but not for artistic or literary cognoscenti. Combine this with a modest amount of self-deprecation, as in: "You know, Greek irregular verbs were so fascinating, I never did get to the chemistry labs."

Other such phrases may be left to the ingenuity of

the clever reader—which you obviously are or you wouldn't be reading this book. Learn to depend upon your specialty: an expert in sports could toss off a line like, "I was too busy watching my backhand to worry about the math involved."

Still and all, our world gets more mathematical and more mechanical every day. It's nice to be au courant with at least some of it.

1. The English writer C. P. Snow indicated that no one could be considered educated who did not know the second law of thermodynamics. What is it?
   a. Popularly, "Heat flows downhill"
   b. Entropy is immutable
   c. The rate of cooling of a body is proportional to the temperature difference between it and its surroundings

2. What is the first law of thermodynamics?
   a. When heat flows across the lines of magnetic force, an electromotive force is created in the mutually perpendicular direction
   b. For every action there is an equal and positive reaction
   c. When mechanical work is transformed into heat, or heat into work, the amount of work is always equivalent to the quantity of heat

3. What was the real significance of Benjamin Franklin's invention of, and experiments with, the lightning rod?
   a. He discovered electricity and its properties

b. It was the first time a provable cause-and-effect relationship had been established for a scientific phenomenon
c. It was the first time that any mechanical power was controlled

4. Oliver Wendell Holmes, the writer, was also a physician. He was responsible for introducing a major advance in medical practice into the United States. What was it?
   a. Open-heart surgery
   b. The idea that doctors must wash their hands before delivering babies
   c. Anesthesia

5. Who discovered penicillin, the first commercial antibiotic?
   a. Dr. Waxman
   b. Dr. Ehrlich
   c. Dr. Fleming

6. Who discovered the function of the heart and the circulation of the blood?
   a. Galileo
   b. Michelangelo
   c. Dr. William Harvey

7. What botanist was the first to classify all living things by genus and species?
   a. Carolus Linnaeus
   b. William Poinsett
   c. William Magnus

8. Who was Aesculapius?
   a. The physician who cured Alexander the Great of typhoid
   b. A Greek ruler who founded a medical school
   c. The Greek god of medicine

9. Some of the most important "laws" now known are Newton's laws of motion. Six statements are listed below. Identify the three laws of motion and take 2 credits for each one.
   a. A body remains in a state of rest or uniform motion in a straight line unless compelled by some external force acting upon it to change that state
   b. The coefficient of friction is the ratio of force required to move one surface over another, to the total force pressing them together
   c. A change in motion is proportional to the force causing the change and takes place in the direction in which the force is acting, or the increase or decrease in velocity is proportional to the force
   d. Moment of inertia is a measure of mass in rotation
   e. Momentum is the quantity of motion measured by the product of mass and velocity
   f. To every action there is always an equal and opposite or contrary reaction

10. A revision of the periodic table developed by Mendeleev regarding elements was done by Moseley. What does it state?

    a. The properties of elements are periodic func-
       tions of the squares of their atomic numbers
    b. The properties of elements are periodic func-
       tions of their densities
    c. Within the elastic limit of any body the ratio of
       the stress to the strain produced is constant

11. What is the Fibonacci series in mathematics?
    a. The rules of harmonic motion
    b. Another name for the Pythagorean series
    c. The sequence in which each number equals
       the sum of the preceding two numbers

12. Marie and Pierre Curie won a Nobel Prize in
1903. For what was it awarded?
    a. The discovery of the X-ray machine
    b. Their work in radioactivity
    c. Their discovery of certain new laws of motion

13. Marie Curie won another Nobel Prize, in a different field, in 1911. At that time she was the first person ever to win two Nobel Prizes. What was the
achievement for which the second one was given?
    a. The development of the theory of entropy
    b. The isolation of metallic radium
    c. The isolation of a new element

14. Eminent husband-and-wife research teams are
fairly rare. Another such pair shared a Nobel Prize
(with B. A. Houssay) for research into carbohydrate
metabolism and enzymes (2 points extra credit for
both names).

    a. Drs. Lunt and Fontanne, in 1963
    b. Drs. Merck and Sharpe, in 1925
    c. Drs. C. F. and Gerty T. Cori, in 1947

15. For what was Archimedes actually looking when his inspiration caused him to shout "Eureka" in his bathtub?
    a. The soap
    b. A means of measuring the weight of any object by the displacement of water
    c. A means of measuring the density of gold

16. What is the Pythagorean Theorem?
    a. Heat capacity is the quantity of heat required to increase the temperature of a system one degree of temperature
    b. $E = MC^3$
    c. The sum of the squares of the two sides of a right-angled triangle is equal to the square of the hypotenuse

17. What is the basic principle of the quantum theory of physics?
    a. The thermal capacity of a substance and its dependence on temperature
    b. Power is the time rate at which work is done
    c. The emission and absorption by atoms and by subatomic particles of light and energy are not continuous but occur in finite steps

18. What is the overall name, geologically speaking, for the current era?

   a. Cenozoic
   b. Mesozoic
   c. Nuclear

19. How did the Celsius and Fahrenheit thermometers get their names?
   a. From the names of the two inventors
   b. From the original manufacturers of these thermometers
   c. From the towns in which the thermometers were invented

20. For whom is the Kelvin scale named, and what is it?
   a. The Kelvin company, makers of electrical appliances
   b. A town in England
   c. William Thompson

21. In the simplest form possible, what is trigonometry?
   a. The measurement of the sides and angles of triangles, particularly the ratio of certain pairs of sides
   b. The study of the motion of heat to surrounding bodies
   c. A form of geology

22. A recent field of study in geology, known as plate tectonics, is considered one of the most important

theories developed in this century. What does it involve?
   a. A shift in the water currents of the earth
   b. A study of the "greenhouse" effect
   c. A study of the shift of land masses

23. What is geometry?
   a. A branch of mathematics which deals with space, the properties of space, and the relations of figures within that space
   b. A branch of mathematics that deals with two-dimensional properties of objects, and their studies
   c. A branch of mathematics that deals with the conversion of two-dimensional representations into three-dimensional drawings

24. Who set up the basic axioms which are the foundation of Euclidean geometry today?
   a. Euclid
   b. Pythagoras
   c. Leonardo da Vinci, while living at Euclid, Greece

25. Geodetic surveying is an important advance in mapping the world. What is the difference between geodetic surveying and plane surveying?
   a. Plane surveying considers the earth as a horizontal plane and geodetic surveying involves distances so large that the curvature of the earth must be taken into account

    b. Plane surveying is work done in an office and geodetic surveying is done in the field

    c. Plane surveying is done from an airplane and geodetic surveying from the ground

26. What is algebra?
    a. The branch of mathematics in which the basic operations of mathematics are generalized
    b. The branch of mathematics in which letters are used for numbers
    c. The branch of mathematics developed by the Arabs

27. Who is generally considered to have developed the foundation for modern astronomy?
    a. Galileo
    b. Copernicus
    c. Erasmus

28. Galileo Galilei found himself in difficulties over his view of the solar system. What did he think and what happened to him?
    a. He thought the earth revolved around the sun and was tried in court
    b. He thought the sun revolved around the earth, and quarreled with the astronomers of his day
    c. He thought the world was coming to an end shortly, and started a religious revival

29. Who developed the first model of the adding machine, and when?

a. Henry Ford, in 1892
b. Cyrus McCormick, in 1860
c. Blaise Pascal, in 1642

30. Although, popularly, Robert Fulton is credited with the invention of the steamboat, another American had a passenger line running much earlier out of Philadelphia. Who was it?
a. Benjamin Franklin
b. Robert Morris
c. John Fitch

31. Who designed the Brooklyn Bridge?
a. Washington Roebling
b. John A. Roebling
c. Ulysses S. Grant

32. Who invented the balloon as a means of manned flight?
a. Montgolfier brothers
b. William Z. Ballon
c. Napoleon, for his army

33. The stock ticker is extremely important to business today. Who invented it?
a. An employee of Merrill Lynch, in 1920
b. Thomas A. Edison, in 1870
c. Henry Ford, in 1921

34. A satellite is placed in geosynchronous orbit at 22,300 miles (i.e., a period of 24 hours for the satellite). Why can't it be another distance?

a. It can be—we haven't done it
b. That is the extreme limit of the delivery system
c. That distance is the only one possible, according to Kepler's third law of planetary motion

35. We are all familiar with the rising and falling sound a train whistle makes as the train approaches the observer and moves away. What is the effect called, and what causes it?
   a. The Doppler effect: as the distance between a source of wave motion and an observer decreases, the frequency increases, and as the distance increases, the frequency decreases
   b. The gravitational effect, caused by the gravitational pull against the molecules
   c. The Kepler effect, caused by differing degrees of the speed of sound

36. James D. Watson, Maurice H. F. Wilkins, and Francis H. C. Crick received a Nobel Prize in 1962. What was the importance of their work?
   a. They found the location of chromosomes
   b. They found the "double helix" structure of deoxyribonucleic acid
   c. They predicted the appearance, via periodicity, of certain stars

37. Wilhelm Roentgen received a Nobel Prize in 1901 for a major discovery. What was it?
   a. The X-ray

b. The curative effects of radiography against malignancies
c. The law of the photoelectric effect

38. Who is generally considered the developer of the quantum theory?
    a. Dr. Compton
    b. Marie Curie
    c. Max Planck

39. Albert Einstein received a Nobel Prize, but not for his theory of relativity. He received it in Physics in 1921 for something different. What was it?
    a. A reanalysis of the laws of motion
    b. A rearrangement of the laws of thermodynamics
    c. The law of the photoelectric effect

40. Why is Halley's Comet called Halley's Comet?
    a. Named after Dr. Edmund Halley, who predicted its next appearance
    b. Named after Halley, England, where the inhabitants rioted in 1682
    c. That is the old French word for "comet," as it appeared in its earliest records

41. Why are ballpoint pens called Biros in many countries?
    a. Slang for fountain pen
    b. Put out by the Biro company
    c. Invented by Ladislao Biro, an Argentinian

42. What basic discovery caused a great deal of interest initially in "seeing by telegraph" (television)?
    a. The discovery of electricity
    b. The discovery of the laws of thermodynamics
    c. The discovery that there was a variation in the electrical conductivity of selenium when exposed to light

43. Allan M. Cormack and Godfrey N. Hounsfield won a Nobel Prize for the CAT scan. Just what is a CAT scan?
    a. Chromographic Altered Topography
    b. Computerized Axial Tomography
    c. Conducted Alternate Treatment

44. Dennis Gabor received the Nobel Prize in Physics in 1971 for the development of a major breakthrough in a certain type of photographic imagery. What was it?
    a. Instant pictures
    b. Color photography
    c. Holographic three-dimensional imagery

45. Willard F. Libby advanced the fields of archaeology, chemistry, and geology with an invention. What was it?
    a. Tree-ring dating of remains
    b. A new method of finding ruins via aerial photography
    c. The "atomic time clock," which determines the age of objects by measuring the radioactive decay of their components

46. Most people have seen F numbers on camera lenses. What do the numbers, or F stops, represent?
   a. The ratio of the focal length to the effective diameter
   b. The initial of the inventor of the modern 35-mm camera, used as a convenient measure
   c. The length of the lens, that is, wide-angle, normal, or telephoto

47. What was the basic invention that revolutionized road-making, and thus also revolutionized road transportation?
   a. The development of concrete that could be poured in panels
   b. Surveyors' instruments which facilitated level roads
   c. Macadamizing, which sealed road surfaces

48. What was the difference between the telephone developed by Alexander Graham Bell and the earlier, unsuccessful attempts of many others?
   a. His worked
   b. His used wires that were connected to a central system, instead of wireless, which could be interfered with
   c. He used an electrical current of fluctuating intensity and frequency, generated by mirroring the acoustic characteristics of sound waves

49. When and where was the first sustained nuclear chain reaction (fission of uranium isotope U 235)?
   a. In 1944, in Peenemünde, Germany

b. In August 1945, at Hiroshima
c. In 1942, at the University of Chicago

50. Exactly what is the Braille system?
    a. A series of raised dots that are exactly the shape of letters and numbers
    b. Recordings for the blind
    c. A system of 6 raised points in 63 combinations (developed by Louis Braille)

TOTAL POINTS POSSIBLE: 55

YOUR SCORE _____

Knowing Whowhatwherewhen (and when not)

The inclusions in this chapter are at least partly happenstantial. Getting your name into history is partly a matter of being in the right place at the right time, and partly a matter of having the right name. Consider, for example, photography. Mr. Niepce had just as much to do with it as did Mr. Daguerre. Unfortunately, he did not have a name that lends itself to pronunciation, and so we have daguerreotypes and not niepceotypes. Mr. Silhouette's name seems to have been made for the use to which it has been put. Doesn't it just sound like what it is?

While it is no longer as fashionable as it once was to memorize dates of famous events, there is a certain éclat in knowing them. How nice to be able to toss into the conversation your awareness that Sir Walter Raleigh saw Pocahontas. How erudite to be aware that the same queen who sent Columbus on his voyage to the New World also tossed the last of the Moors out during her time as ruler of Spain. Shakespeare might well have talked to someone who had known a Moor, and thus received the inspiration for Othello.

Even if they haven't been there, most people will sigh dreamily at the mention of Paris or Venice. But why not be unique and bring Timbuktu into the conversation instead? A knowledge of people and places will permit you to drop an occasional reference to the Grand Canal. You might go so far as to declare, "Not *that* Grand Canal. I was talking about the Grand Canal from Wuxi to Suzhou, of course." If you're looking for a conversation stopper, this is practically guaranteed. There may well be a spoilsport in the crowd who has been to Urumchi, in which case the proper reply would be, "Oh, yes, we considered it, but it's getting a bit touristy."

There is also a certain appeal in being able to discuss little-known battles. When the talk turns to battles of the past (or even the present, unfortunately), a quick allusion to the battle of Lepanto as being far more significant than anything being discussed is apt to create a favorable impression. The odds are probably two to one that your listeners haven't the faintest idea of the battle of Lepanto, but with a casual reference you present yourself as someone with a firm grasp of military and political history. (To save you a trip to the encyclopedia, the battle of Lepanto—October 7, 1571—prevented the Ottoman Empire from taking over the whole Mediterranean.)

But what is the value to you, apart from being able to hold your own in a company that does not consist of geographers or historians? It's an advantage, when traveling, to know where you are and what has happened there. It makes the otherwise very dull spot a few miles outside Waterloo much more interesting when you know about the battle of Waterloo. However, we strongly suggest skipping Waterloo. It is an eminently forgettable spot, unless you like looking at an empty field with some low mounds on it.

One of those happy accidents of fate—or unhappy accidents, depending on your point of view—occurred at the Mandelbaum Gate. The name has been immortalized, simply because the place and the name came together at a significant moment in history.

Do not hesitate to look up some other little-known places, or people, or events, not included in this chapter. There is nothing like being a specialist in some area, and the more obscure, probably, the better. Much can be gained by knowing a good deal about the life of someone whose name sounds vaguely familiar but is not immediately identifiable. For example, one of us has a dear friend whose pet hate is being asked his name when he telephones a business office. He now tells the inquirer that he is Millard Fillmore. The average telephone operator, receptionist, or call recipient knows the sound of Millard Fillmore, knows that he or she has heard the name before, and knows that it was somebody reasonably important. The calls always go through promptly, at which point the quondam Millard Fillmore identifies himself accurately. If everybody knew about Millard Fillmore this wouldn't work, but since hardly anyone does, it is entirely successful. Knowing a little bit about Millard Fillmore has saved this ingenious gentleman hours of waiting at the other end of the telephone.

From such ingenuity is a form of culture created. Not only did this man find out about Millard Fillmore, but we are sure that his telephone contacts have been similarly enlightened.

In this manner, someone with rather easily acquired cultural facts about a little-known person can make himself (or herself) the center of an interested audience. We are sure that readers of this book will be able to devise an equally useful plan for utilizing the facts that they may discover by reading this chapter. Again, we have given you suggestions, examples, the raw material for success; the rest lies with you, your wit and your ingenuity.

You may, perhaps, find yourself immortalized for something that was really not your responsibility, as did the eponymous Mr. Mandelbaum. All he did was own the building that became the official boundary between Israel and Jordan before the Six-Day War. The rest of his story is lost to history.

1. Which Egyptian pharaoh is considered a monotheist, in that he tried to establish a religion in which the sun alone was the god to worship?
    a. Akhenaten

  b. Rameses I
  c. Nefertiti

2. Who were the Etruscans?
  a. Early Greek settlers
  b. Early Spaniards
  c. Italian natives before the Romans

3. What was the permanent, long-range effect of the battle of Marathon?
  a. The Marathon races were made part of the Olympics
  b. The Trojans lost the war
  c. The Greeks defeated the Persians permanently

4. Who was Frederick Barbarossa, and what was the meaning of his sobriquet?
  a. A wicked king, called Blackbeard
  b. The Spanish conqueror of southern France, noted for his barbarity
  c. Frederick I of Germany, known as Redbeard

5. After what was the region of France now called Provence named?
  a. A town near Rome
  b. The local mountains
  c. The word for "province" in Latin

6. Exactly what is the Magna Carta (or Magna Charta)?

   a. All the laws of England compiled in one book
   b. The laws the Norman conquerors brought
      over from France
   c. The first document in English history contain-
      ing the idea that the king was subject to cer-
      tain laws

7. What is the Domesday Book?
   a. The criminal code of early Europe
   b. The list of prison terms and fines imposed on
      the conquered British
   c. A list of all landholdings and buildings, ex-
      ecuted by William the Conqueror

8. King George I of England had one particular
problem in communicating with his ministers and his
people. It was a major and significant difficulty. What
was it?
   a. He was deaf
   b. He could neither read nor write
   c. He couldn't speak English

9. Charlemagne had a permanent effect on the universities of Western Europe. What did he do?
   a. He forbade any universities and retarded the
      growth of schools on the Continent
   b. He imported scholars from the Near East to
      set up universities
   c. He set up, through an appointee, the liberal
      arts system that remained in effect for hun-
      dreds of years

10. There are two Winston Churchills, contemporaries, in most encyclopedias. Who was the "other" Churchill?
   a. A poor cousin, who also wrote books
   b. A correspondent in the Spanish-American War
   c. An (apparently) unrelated American novelist

11. For what is the village of Oberammergau famous?
   a. The winter Olympics
   b. "Silent Night" was composed there
   c. The Passion play

12. What is the actual name of Buddha, as far as we can tell?
   a. Siddhartha Gautama
   b. Kung Tai Jai
   c. Buddha

13. Avicenna, an Arabian, had a marked influence on European education in a major field. What was it?
   a. Medicine
   b. Natural history
   c. Philosophy

14. *Guide for the Perplexed,* written in the twelfth century, and formulating a proof of the existence of God, was written by a Jewish philosopher. It has had

great influence over not only Jewish theological
thought but also Christian theology. Who was the
author?
   a. Spinoza
   b. Descartes
   c. Maimonides

15. Who were the first mother-in-law and father-in-
law of Henry VIII?
   a. Katharine of Aragon and Philip of Castile
   b. Ferdinand and Isabella of Spain
   c. Louis XIV and Queen Anne

16. Where is Chichén Itzá and what is it?
   a. In France, the site of prehistoric caves
   b. In South America, the site of Aztec culture
   c. In Mexico, the site of Mayan culture

17. The layout of Paris that we see today is chiefly
the work of one man. Who was he?
   a. Le Corbusier
   b. Baron Haussmann
   c. M. Filimori

18. The gardens of Versailles, and of many other
French palaces and chateaus, are all in the style and
form established by one man. Who was he?
   a. Capability Brown
   b. Antonio Gaudí
   c. Lenôtre

19. For what are the "Five Towns" in England particularly noted?
    a. Scenery
    b. Pottery and china industry
    c. Tapestry weaving

20. "Quai d'Orsay" is frequently used in referring to one branch of the French government. Which branch is it, and why?
    a. Criminal investigation division—main prison
    b. Navy—its main offices are on a quay
    c. Foreign office—location of headquarters

21. Iceland has glaciers, but it is really not that icy. Why is it called Iceland?
    a. It was formerly ice-covered
    b. The name means "island"
    c. Explorers reached the north side of the island and saw only the glaciers

22. What is known as the "Ring of Fire"?
    a. The volcanoes in Alaska
    b. The natural phenomenon known as Saint Elmo's fire
    c. The rim of the Pacific, which is ringed with active volcanoes

23. Alfred Dreyfus was tried for treason, convicted, sent to Devils Island, tried again, and finally pardoned. What eventually happened to him?

a. He was reinstated in the French army and eventually became a general
b. He died during his second trial
c. He spent the rest of his life in the U.S.

24. Who is credited with introducing a new type of stage entertainment, the revue, a medley of skits and light pieces, with stage effects and pretty girls? (Originally, there were topical reviews of events of the preceding year, hence the name.)
   a. David Belasco
   b. Billy Rose
   c. Florenz Ziegfeld

25. Who finished *Das Kapital* for Karl Marx?
   a. Lenin
   b. Stalin
   c. Engels

26. What were, or are, sumptuary laws?
   a. Limits on food, imposed during famines
   b. Rules regarding what clothing, jewelry, etc., may be worn by certain classes of people
   c. Limits on spending imposed by Congress against the states

27. What are blue laws?
   a. Laws originally published in a blue-covered book in Puritan America

b. Rigid laws imposed by a Congress under a majority leader named Zachariah Blue

c. Laws regulating business and activities on Sundays

28. From what is the name Zeppelin derived?
  a. Count Ferdinand von Zeppelin made the first craft of this type
  b. Invented in the city of Zeppel
  c. ZEP are the initials of the German words meaning lighter than air

29. What incident triggered World War I?
  a. Assassination of Czar Alexander II
  b. Assassination of General von Bülow
  c. Assassination of Archduke Francis Ferdinand at Sarajevo

30. What was the Maginot Line (in World War II)?
  a. Defenses between France and Spain
  b. Defenses between France and Germany
  c. Defenses between Germany and Poland

31. Who was the leader of the French faction that collaborated with the Germans after the fall of France in World War II, and where was his government headquarters?
  a. Pétain, at Vichy

b. Foch, at Paris
c. Quisling, at Nice

32. What was the status of the country now known
as Korea (or the countries now called North and
South Korea) prior to World War II?
   a. Same as now
   b. Belonged to China
   c. Ruled by Japan since 1910

33. Charles Martel (Charles the Hammer), the
grandfather of Charlemagne, was the victor at the
battle of Tours, in 732 A.D. This is considered one of
the most significant military events in European history. Why?
   a. Started the Middle Ages
   b. Stopped the Moors of Spain, who never
      reached any farther
   c. Stopped Charlemagne permanently

34. Who was Button Gwinnett?
   a. A legendary figure in the Civil War
   b. The founder of Boston
   c. A signer of the Declaration of Independence,
      whose signature is very rare

35. What was the Yalta Agreement, so called because it was made at the Yalta Conference in Febru-
ary 1945?
      a. Divided Berlin and provided agreement for
         Russia to enter war against Japan

b. Took Cuba away from the U.S.

c. Gave Puerto Rico to the U.S.

36. The Morrill Act of 1862 was one of the most important pieces of legislation ever passed in connection with American higher education. Why?
    a. Set up teacher-training schools in the U.S.
    b. Established the land-grant colleges in the U.S.
    c. Provided for universal compulsory education

37. Bonnie Prince Charlie is a celebrated figure in history, and also in literature. Who was he?
    a. An exceptionally handsome French prince
    b. A Scottish King who fought with Wallace the Bruce
    c. A Stuart claimant to the British throne

38. George Washington served as a colonel in 1753 and 1754. In what war and for whom?
    a. Hundred Years War in France, for the British
    b. In the Caribbean, during the defense of Jamaica, for the U.S.
    c. In the French and Indian Wars, for the British

39. When someone describes a project as a "Potemkin village," to what is he referring?
    a. A lovely, prototypical peasant village in Europe
    b. An excellent example of early town planning
    c. A false-front village put up for show only, where nobody lives

40. Eamon de Valera, at one time prime minister of Ireland, was not Irish by birth. Where was he born?
   a. England
   b. France
   c. United States

41. The commander of cavalry who led, in error, the Charge of the Light Brigade has become famous for something else entirely. Who was he and for what is he famous?
   a. The Earl of Sandwich, for sandwiches
   b. Lord Cardigan, for the sweater that bears his name
   c. Lord Wellington, for Wellington boots

42. Which American philosopher is considered as the founder of the educational school known as "progressive education"?
   a. James Kilpatrick
   b. Charles Eliot
   c. John Dewey

43. William Carlos Williams, the doctor poet, composed his most famous work about a city in New Jersey. Which city?
   a. Paterson
   b. Hackensack
   c. Trenton

44. Queen Victoria of England married off her daughters into many of the royal houses of Europe.

Apparently, the women carried a genetic illness with them. What was it?

a. Blindness

b. Diabetes

c. Hemophilia

45. The United States has had only a few Presidents who were not lawyers. Herbert Hoover was one of them. What was his profession?

a. Physician

b. Engineer

c. Military officer

46. Where was the first permanent English settlement in the now United States?

a. Plymouth, Massachusetts

b. Saint Augustine, Florida

c. Jamestown, Virginia

47. Who built, or at least started, the Tower of London?

a. Henry VIII

b. William the Conqueror

c. Queen Elizabeth I

48. On the banks of the Passaic River, in Paterson, New Jersey, there is an invention, or a refinement of an invention, by J. P. Holland. What is it?

a. The first silk mill

b. The first telegraph machine

c. An early submarine

49. William the Conqueror is always thought of as French, but by descent on his father's side, he was not. What was he?
   a. Scandinavian—his grandfather was Norman (Norseman)
   b. Moorish, as his grandfather came from North Africa
   c. English, which is why he felt he had a claim to England

50. According to records and statistics, what is the most literate country in the world?
   a. China
   b. Costa Rica
   c. Iceland

51. Hannibal's crossing of the Alps during the Second Punic War (218–201 B.C.) is considered one of the great military feats of all time. Why?
   a. First time sleds were ever used
   b. Hannibal invented snowshoes for his army
   c. The baggage train and retinue included a herd of elephants, in the snow

52. Heinrich Schliemann is famous as an archaeologist. What was his major discovery?
   a. Prehistoric American Indian paintings
   b. Troy
   c. Roman ruins

53. "The Beautiful Blue Danube" may be the name of the song, but that is not what the river is called in Vienna. What is its name there?
    a. Green Gorge
    b. Donau
    c. Volga

54. What is the Golden Horn?
    a. A valley where a great gold discovery was made
    b. The corner of Mesopotamia where "golden" corn was first grown
    c. The inlet of the Bosporus at Istanbul

55. What is the Great Rift Valley?
    a. The site of the Wupatki crater
    b. The site of Death Valley
    c. An enormous geologic fault in Africa

TOTAL POSSIBLE ANSWERS: 55

YOUR SCORE _____

For the Cultural Elite Only

There is probably not a cultural event worth your tuxedo where you somehow can't reveal your knowledge of one of these gems.

Use them wisely.

1. From what is the exclamation point derived?
   a. Early typefaces had fewer symbols than needed and hence typesetters had to combine such items as single quote marks and periods
   b. Originally called an explanation point, it was used as an indication that an item was particularly important
   c. Derived from the Latin word for "joy"

2. The saucer shape for champagne glasses is no longer favored as much as is the "tulip" shape, but it

was extremely popular for a long time. What is the legend—perhaps a true story—about how the champagne saucer came to be made in that shape?

    a. It was modeled on the shape of Marie Antoinette's breasts

    b. It was modeled in the shape of a cut grape, as the most appropriate shape for a sparkling wine

    c. Since the champagne process was developed in a monastery, the glass was made in the shape of the glasses they used

3. What is the motto usually seen on sundials? An extra 2 points if you can give it in the original Latin.

    a. "I count none but sunny hours"; or: "I count no hours but sunny ones"

    b. "Time passes"

    c. "Art is long and Time is fleeting"

4. One of the largest natural disasters in history took place in this century. What was it?

    a. The explosion of Mount Saint Helens

    b. Hurricane Diane

    c. The flood of the Huang He River in China

5. Many of the European languages are called Romance languages, as they are related to the Roman language, Latin. Which of the following languages is *not* a Romance language?

    a. Rumanian

    b. English
    c. Portuguese

6. One of Dante Gabriel Rossetti's most famous works, his *Poems,* disappeared for several years, until the only copy was made available again. Where had it been?
    a. His publisher had lost it
    b. It had been buried in his wife's grave and then dug up
    c. He had given away the poems to a friend and had to sue to get them back

7. Where would you go to find wild goldfish, or goldfish in a native state?
    a. They exist, in all their red or gold glory, in streams in China
    b. There are no goldfish, as we know them, in the wild state
    c. They come from cold mountain streams in the islands of the South Pacific

8. Why are the hands on most sample clocks set at 8:18?
    a. In honor of the time of Lincoln's death
    b. In honor of the Declaration of Independence
    c. That form offers the most advertising space

9. Why do barber poles have red and white stripes?
    a. For patriotic reasons, as there are also blue stripes

b. The red represents blood, the white bandages, since barbers were once surgeons

c. To make the signs highly visible

10. From what did the name badminton (for a game played with a bat and a shuttlecock) come?

a. From the name of the village in India where the game was first played

b. From the name of the person who invented the game

c. From Badminton, the home of the Duke of Beaufort, who first used shuttlecocks

11. What does the phrase "of that ilk" mean? (Or what did it mean originally?)

a. It means that the individual's name matches that of his "seat" or home, as Smith of Smith Hall; its secondary meaning, now most used, means "of that same type"

b. It indicates that a man is an associate of evil people, without saying so in a way that can be brought to court

c. It is complimentary, meaning that the person so described is of high character

12. Who was "The Man in the Iron Mask"?

a. A twin brother of Louis XIV

b. An illegitimate son of one of the French kings, who had tried to claim the throne

c. No ironclad evidence really exists

13. Why is a gangster sometimes called a thug?
    a. This is a German slang term, adopted by gang-
       sters themselves
    b. Thugs, members of a religious sect in India,
       murdered in honor of the goddess Kali
    c. It represents the sound of a victim falling to
       the ground

14. Is a zebra white with black stripes or the reverse?
    a. A zebra is neither, as the stripes alternate and
       there is no background
    b. White with black stripes
    c. Black with white stripes

15. Is the sun nearer to the earth in summer or in
winter?
    a. The sun is nearer in winter, but the angle of
       the sun's rays, as the tilt of the earth is in-
       volved, is much more slanted
    b. Obviously, it is nearer in summer
    c. It is the same distance always; it is only the tilt
       of the earth that is different

16. From what did the word "bedlam" come?
    a. It is a corrupt form of the word "babel," mean-
       ing a confusion of tongues
    b. It has been corrupted from Bethlehem Hospi-
       tal, a London madhouse
    c. It came from an old poem about a fool, Tom
       of Bedlam

17. Who was "the little woman who started the big war"?
    a. Helen of Troy
    b. Julia Ward Howe
    c. Harriet Beecher Stowe

18. What is the oldest university (that we know actually existed)?
    a. Padua in Italy
    b. One founded by Alexander the Great
    c. One founded by Socrates in Greece

19. What ear led to a major war?
    a. Napoleon, who had hearing problems, declared war when his ministers had recommended against such a step but he hadn't heard them
    b. Julius Caesar had an ear infection and lost a major battle
    c. Captain Robert Jenkins claimed he had his ear cut off by the Spaniards, and his appeal to Parliament led eventually to the War of the Austrian Succession (which started as the War of Jenkins' Ear)

20. What is the common factor in the history of all U.S. Presidents inaugurated before 1837 (and not that they were all thirty-five years old or more).
    a. They were all married for the second time

b. They all died on July 4
c. They had all been born in a foreign country.

TOTAL SCORE POSSIBLE: 22

YOUR SCORE _____

Answers
(which the truly cultured may skip)

1. b. On Mount Olympus. However, since no one who has climbed the mountain has found used thunderbolt holders or empty nectar containers, the matter is open for discussion.

2. g. Pyramids of Egypt; h. Gardens of Semiramis at Babylon; i. Statue of Zeus at Olympia, by Phidias; j. Temple of Diana (or Artemis) at Ephesus; k. Mausoleum at Halicarnassus; l. Colossus at Rhodes; and either m. Pharos of Egypt, n. Walls of Babylon, or o. Palace of Cyprus. 1 extra point for any correct over 4—total 3 extra points.

3. c. They are the historical and mythological traditions of Scandinavian and Teutonic history, mainly Icelandic and Norwegian, from approximately the twelfth century. The term is now used for almost any heroic tale.

4. c. This is the "Hall of the Dead." Here Odin (Wotan) feasts every night, with the slain heroes, on mead and boar's meat, and from here every morning they all go out to battle. The Valkyries, despite any ideas to the contrary, wait on them.

5. a. Paul Bunyan, of American folklore.

6. b. Rabelais trained as a physician and practiced for most of his adult life.

7. c. Confucius.

8. c. They were written in English, and gave literary works in the native language of the country, which was English, respectability. Chaucer had been

writing about French and Italian themes, and this was an English book on English themes.

9. c. This was a book of advice and guidance for the dead, with instructions to help them find their way to the afterlife. It is written in hieroglyphics.

10. c. Al Borak is the horse that carried Mohammed to seventh heaven and was then received into Paradise. It had the wings of an eagle, spoke with the voice of a man, and glittered with light.

11. c. *The Vagabond King,* by Rudolf Friml, still performed occasionally as an operetta, and whose songs are still popular. While Villon existed, the exploits described never happened, as far as can be determined. Villon is most famous for his "Ballad of Lost Ladies," which contains the line, "But where are the snows of yesteryear?"

12. c. The group was in Florence, which was being attacked by the plague in 1348. They hoped that by shutting themselves up and staying away from everyone else, they would be spared.

13. a. It was written in Latin, which was still used in the sixteenth century for learned works, no matter what the native language of the writer. This permitted the work to be read by scholars all over the Western world, and eliminated the need for translations.

14. c. Sherlock Holmes. There is no such address, but a reproduction of his living room has been constructed in a nearby pub.

15. c. This was a fifty-volume set of 418 literary selections made by Dr. Charles W. Eliot, president emeritus of Harvard. He considered these works to

be "the essentials of a liberal education." It was also known as the Harvard Classics.

16. b. *David Copperfield.* Dickens himself had been forced, because of his father's debts, to work in a factory when he was very young.

17. c. When they were originally written, especially in Germany in the eighteenth century, they were always set in backgrounds that included Gothic architecture. This was usually a castle out in a wilderness, with plenty of secret passages, long dark corridors, and mysterious corners.

18. b. Mrs. Malaprop. A malapropism is a word used wrongly to humorous effect.

19. c. She ran away with Paris to Troy, although she was married to the king of Sparta. She was supposed to be outstandingly beautiful: "Was this the face that launched a thousand ships . . . ?"

20. c. Scylla was a sea monster and Charybdis a whirlpool, on opposite sides of the Strait of Messina, and representing equal dangers to the sailors who attempted to pass between them. (It is believed the sea monster was actually a sharp hidden rock.)

21. c. He died of a hemorrhage, while acting in his play *Le Malade Imaginaire (The Imaginary Invalid).*

22. c. Durante Alighieri, known as Dante, is best remembered for *The Divine Comedy,* a complete philosophical system in verse.

23. c. A sonnet is always fourteen lines of iambic verse in five feet. There is the Shakespearean sonnet —three quatrains with six alternating rhymes and a detached rhymed couplet—and the form used by

Keats, Milton, and others, called the Italian sonnet. This consists of a rhyme scheme that runs a-b-b-a, a-b-b-a and an additional six lines that may be rhymed in various ways.

24. a. *Crime and Punishment.*

25. c. The Grail, or Holy Grail, is traditionally the cup or chalice used by Christ at the Last Supper. The search for the Grail is the main theme of the Arthurian legends. Another story says it was a dish from which the Paschal Lamb was served, but most traditions call it a cup or chalice.

26. c. Heep keeps insisting how " 'umble" he is, but he is actually a sneak and a malicious planner of destruction for others.

27. c. & d. Basically, Osiris, and Isis, his wife, although there were hundreds including Anubis and Ra, Amon, and sometimes Horus.

28. c. A gnome or a house spirit, in German folklore. It is the equivalent, approximately, of a brownie.

29. c. The brothers Grimm were world-renowned philologists. They worked out, among many other things, Grimm's law on the permutation of consonants. (No further explanation will be given here; it is far too complicated.)

30. c. Among the famous writers who gathered at the Algonquin were Dorothy Parker and Robert Benchley.

31. b. Mr. Hyde.

32. a. Don Quixote de la Mancha (he is the original "Man of La Mancha").

33. a. & d. *The Three Musketeers* and *Twenty Years After;* also *The Count of Monte Cristo, The Viscount of Bragelonne* (the latter is sometimes split into several novels, including *The Man in the Iron Mask*), or any of many others.

34. c. Ruritania, now used almost generically for any mythical romantic country.

35. c. In Transylvania. It is said that the castle that reputedly belonged to him was the model for castles in the various Disney parks, but other castles have also claimed this honor.

36. c. "The Lady of the Lake," by Sir Walter Scott (canto II, stanza 10).

37. c. The *Rubáiyát of Omar Khayyám*, as translated by Edward Fitzgerald.

38. c. "Elegy in a Country Churchyard," by Thomas Gray (stanza 19).

39. c. Rudyard Kipling, "The Betrothed."

40. c. Jean de La Fontaine. His *Contes,* or *Fables,* became so popular in France that many of the tapestry works made illustrations of his stories, and the morals have passed into French as well as English literature.

41. c. The dragon.

42. c. The Vedas are the four sacred books of the Brahmins. They consist of prayers, hymns, and incantations, in verse and in prose.

43. c. The novels are written in the technique known as "stream of consciousness" and involve experiments in language and the making of new words to express a particular meaning.

44. a. Daniel Defoe's *Journal of the Plague Year,* written about half a century later, is considered far more explanatory and evocative.

45. c. Arachne was a girl of Lydia, in ancient Greece, who challenged Minerva to surpass her in weaving. Minerva changed her to a spider.

46. c. Washington Irving invented the character of Diedrich Knickerbocker for his stories of old New York. The name was picked up quickly and Father Knickerbocker has been a symbol of New York City ever since. The original illustrations, by George Cruickshank, showed men with very loose trousers, in the old Dutch style. These became popular, considerably later, and were called knickerbockers.

47. c. A form of Japanese poetry in three lines, the first with five syllables, the second with seven, and the third with five, the whole presenting a complete picture or evoking a mood.

48. c. These were the pen names of Anne, Emily, and Charlotte Brontë.

49. c. He was chiefly noted for his writings on New England Puritanism.

50. c. They were expelled from Nova Scotia. Many settled around New Orleans, where the name became altered to Cajun. Nova Scotia is called Acadie in French.

Art, art, and (art)

1. c. Northern Spain, particularly at Altamira, and the valley of the Dordogne in France contain several hundred caves with paintings. Lascaux, the most famous, is now closed to tourists because of damage to the paintings, but a replica has been built nearby.

2. c. Egyptian art did not use perspective.

3. c. We are fairly sure they were carved from tree trunks. The forms are rigid, and are circumscribed by what would be the dimensions of the trunk.

4. c. Scraps of paint have been found often enough to indicate that the Greeks painted their statutes and often their buildings in bright colors. The pure white statues we see now are not what the Greeks originally saw.

5. c. Lord Elgin, the British ambassador to the sultan of Turkey, got permission in 1801 to take the frieze to London in order to keep it safe. This he did, and there they are.

6. c. The Romans seem to have invented concrete, an absolute essential for large structures such as the Colosseum.

7. c. It is locked by the keystone, placed in the top of the arch, which is round.

8. c. The flying buttress pushes inward, thus relieving the pillars, which support the roof, from its outward push, for the roof, which is stone, is very heavy.

9. b. The Van Eyck brothers of Flanders are generally considered to be the inventors of oil as a painting base.

10. c. The Medici.

11. c. Hans Holbein. We know King Henry VIII and his courtiers, in a visual way, chiefly through Holbein's paintings and sketches. Holbein, incidentally, was born in Germany, but considered himself Swiss, as he lived in Switzerland.

12. c. Carrara marble, quarried near the city of that name in central Italy, is particularly white and beautiful.

13. c. This is a highly complicated kind of architectural ornament superimposed on Gothic. It started in the Iberian Peninsula, but was rapidly exported to Latin America, where it can be seen in its startling full-bloom on the many highly decorated cathedral facades.

14. c. The original painting showed the officers of a militia company at noon, leaving their armory. The painting was hung in a room that was filled with peat smoke on many occasions, and was so darkened that it was believed to be a night picture.

15. c. He was the first, and possibly the greatest, of the landscape gardeners who developed the English garden.

16. c. Viollet-le-Duc, who put his own face on one of the statues on the roof of Notre Dame cathedral. There has been considerable criticism that what we now see is his idea of what Notre Dame should be, and not that of the original builders.

17. c. James McNeill Whistler.

18. c. Claude Monet called a painting of a sunset *An Impression.*

19. c. This group was originally seven men who agreed, in 1848, to try to get away from machine work and return to the craft ideals of earlier times. They included William Morris, who gave his name to the Morris chair, Dante Gabriel Rossetti, and others.

20. b. Frank Lloyd Wright.

21. c. Buckminster Fuller.

22. c. The French style is formal and symmetrical; the English tries to be more natural.

23. c. Genre painting portrays everyday life and common subjects, as opposed to noble subjects and idealized backgrounds.

24. c. It is a method of painting in which watercolors are mixed with water and gum.

25. c. It is built in the form of a spiral ramp, on the walls of which the art is exhibited. Visitors start at the top and walk down the ramp, viewing as they go. (They can, of course, walk up, but very few people do.)

26. b. The supporting construction is on the outside. The exoskeleton, painted brilliant colors, is made part of the visual effect of the building. The Frenchman in the street tends to refer to it as "the gas factory"—*l'usine de gaz*.

27. b. Michelangelo was technically the architect, but Giovanni Bernini did much of the work inside, and also designed the colonnades outside, which are an integral part of the visual design.

28. c. Sir Christopher Wren, who designed most of the churches in the older sections of London.

29. b. No other building is allowed to be higher.

30. a. Rockwell's paintings are among the most-loved American art, and were frequently used as covers for magazines, notably the *Saturday Evening Post*.

31. b. She was Mrs. Giocondo.

32. b.

33. b.

34. c. Engraving, to which he turned more and more in his later years.

35. c. Sculpture.

36. c. Marcel Duchamp, of the Cubist school.

37. c. Frédéric Auguste Bartholdi.

38. c. A Babylonian clay tablet, apparently from 2000–3000 B.C. It is now in the Harvard University museum.

39. b. Gerardus Mercator (Gerhard Kremer), who developed the Mercator projection—a form of drawing that indicates a round object on a flat surface. His method is still used.

40. c. Giovanni Battista Piranesi.

41. b. Gustave Doré.

42. a. Joseph Mallord William Turner. See *Rain, Steam, and Speed,* possibly his most famous painting.

43. a. Hieronymus Bosch.

44. c. The Great Wall of China.

45. c. It was built as a mausoleum for the wife of the shah. Her name was Mumtaz Mahal and she died in 1629.

46. c. Collage.

47. c. Objets trouvés (found objects).

48. c. Pop art.

49. c. Antonio Gaudí.

50. c. The women of the pueblo have developed pottery into a high art form.

51. c. Tapestries. The firm was founded in the sixteenth century by the Gobelin family, and was later taken over by the French government. It is particularly noted for the famous Gobelin blue.

52. c. The chateau of Chenonceaux was built on piers over the river, which made it lovely to look at but extremely damp and cold.

53. c. In the Palace of Versailles, France.

54. c. The Louvre in Paris. It is officially known as *Nike of Samothrace*.

55. a. The Metropolitan Museum of Art, in New York City, contains the reconstituted Temple of Dendur, from Egypt.

Airs and Affectations:
Etiquette and Manners

1. a. The *Deipnosophists*, by Athenaeus, is referred to in every history of food.

2. b. Coelius Apicius wrote a cookbook, called *De Re Culinaria*, supposedly in Roman times (the first copy we have, dated about 1420, is a Latin manuscript).

3. c. This sauce made from fermented fish is reputed to have had what we would call an unpleasant odor.

4. c. In 1855, in preparation for the Exposition Universelle, a committee of wine brokers and exporters classified the Bordeaux wines officially. They classified only the Médoc and Sauternes districts, and their ratings were based on the opinions of their day. Only sixty growths of Médoc were classed, out of nearly a thousand, so that anything classified is considered far superior to anything not classified.

5. a. There are actually four First Growths: Château Lafite (one *t*, please), Château Margaux, Château Latour, and Château Haut-Brion. Many people, including the owners of the château, consider Château Mouton-Rothschild, which almost made this group, to be fully the equal of these four.

6. c. Château d'Yquem is considered to be most superior, with everything else a much poorer second. About this particular classification there is little argument.

7. b. The name comes from Jerez de la Frontera,

in Spain, written Xeres in French, and anglicized to sherry. It is basically a blended wine, mixed with older wines, in the Solera system.

8. a. Wheat has more nitrogenous material and provides a more balanced diet. Potatoes are missing certain essentials.

9. b. As far as we can tell, it was mead, made from honey, or an equivalent. In Greece, this was hydromel, honey that has fermented in approximately ten times its weight of water.

10. c. Tomatoes, potatoes, various capsicum plants (the peppers of the American Southwest, and the white bean used in cassoulet in France, plus many others). The cuisine we now consider typical of the Mediterranean area did not come into use until these vegetables arrived.

11. b. This is a chopped beef patty, broiled. It was prescribed, as more digestible than unchopped beef, by Dr. J. S. Salisbury approximately one hundred years ago, and acquired his name.

12. b. According to *Larousse Gastronomique,* French service involves setting filled plates on the table before the guests sit down, in the old, traditional manner shown in paintings and scenes of the French court. Russian service, which is most customary today, involves passing food to each guest while it is still hot, or arranging the plates in the kitchen and bringing a filled plate to each guest.

13. b. The phylloxera is an insect or plant louse, one of the worst enemies of grapevines. It was accidentally introduced into Europe about 1860, and de-

stroyed 2.5 million acres of vineyards. Since native American vines are resistant to the insect, all the vineyards were replanted with American roots and grafted vines. (Phylloxera did a good deal of damage in California, which then used European rootstocks.) There is a school of thought which holds that pre-phylloxera vines were better, and produced better wine, but this cannot be determined.

14. c. It is a type of wine new to this country, in which fermentation has been stopped by the addition of Cognac. It is quite popular in Europe.

15. b. German whites are excellent and world famous. There are hardly any German red wines.

16. b. This is a wine, often from New York State or California, that is named for the variety of grape from which it is made. This is in contradiction to the basic European practice, which names the wines after the location where they are grown or made. American law permits a varietal name only if 51 percent of the grapes are of the named variety. In Europe, on the other hand, grape varieties in wine districts are limited severely, by both tradition and law. Many place-name wines are, in fact, varietals, although they are not so labeled.

17. a. Brut is the driest champagne. It has 1.5 percent added sugar, plus an old wine base, as against 3 percent sugar for extra dry and 4 percent or more for dry. Despite the fact that many people claim to like very dry champagne, dry is the best seller for many or most champagnes.

18. c. There was an ample supply of taverns and

inns in England and on the Continent throughout the seventeenth and eighteenth centuries. These were not, however, genuine restaurants, with a bill of fare and a wide choice. In 1765, in France, M. Boulanger posted a sign indicating that he served *restaurants,* or restorers. He was attacked by the Caterer's Guild, which sued, but he won his case and opened the first genuine restaurant. After the French Revolution, many unemployed chefs from the great houses opened luxurious restaurants featuring elegant meals.

19. b. Thomas Jefferson, who hired excellent chefs, used tomatoes when almost no one else did, and kept a record of when his vegetables ripened.

20. c. Parmentier wanted the French to grow and eat potatoes, but the people would not cooperate. He thereupon planted a field of potatoes, announced that it was only for the royal table, and posted a guard around it. The guard had instructions to look the other way, and soon potatoes appeared in every garden.

21. c. Catherine de' Medici married the future Henry II of France in 1533. This event is usually credited with heralding the introduction of haute cuisine from Florence, with its luxurious and sophisticated court.

22. c. Marco Polo, following his return from China, but the story is probably not true.

23. a. A dish, now considered quintessentially Scottish, consisting of the heart, lungs, and liver, sometimes the tripe and/or chitterlings, of a sheep or

lamb, made into a pudding and boiled in the maw (stomach) of the animal.

24. b. This seems to be a phonetic rendering of Chinese words meaning "assorted things." It is simply a mixture, and not a recognized part of Chinese cuisine.

25. b. Couscous, a semolina dish in which the grains are steamed, with vegetables and meat, usually lamb, added. The grain is groats, from wheat, and the lamb is sometimes mutton.

26. c. The meats are raw. The first two are cured, but carpaccio is not.

27. b. He was probably looking for spices, as were others. The fall of Constantinople in 1453 cut off access to spices, badly needed in a time of no refrigeration.

28. b. A trencher was originally the thick slice of bread used for a plate. A good trencherman apparently ate the plate as well as the food on it.

29. b. It really means "with a crust," and refers to dishes baked until a little crust forms. The crust may or may not include cheese, but many of us got our first experience with macaroni au gratin, which always had cheese.

30. c. Dom Perignon, the blind cellarmaster of the Abbey of Hautvillers. In 1668 he adopted the use of corks to close the bottles, which held in the secondary fermentation that made it bubbly. (He is popularly credited with exclaiming, "Come quick, I am drinking stars!" when he first tasted champagne.)

31. b. Nouvelle cuisine is designed not for dieting,

but for lightness and to get away from the heavy sauces, made with flour, and the elaborate preparations of classic cuisine. Cuisine minceur is diet food, deliberately low calorie and intended to be eaten by those who are trying to lose weight. Nouvelle cuisine has also come to be noted for its unusual pairings of food, its use of new and exotic fruits, and, frequently, the artistic arrangement of the food on the plates prior to serving.

32. a. As far as we can tell, a lentil soup or stew.

33. b. Maize. All other grains are called corn. The *Oxford English Dictionary* says the term "corn" is applied collectively to all the cereal plants.

34. c. Hock is the British term for what is called Rhine wine in the U.S., or if made in America, probably Johannisberg Riesling and Sylvaner. Almost any U.S.-made white wine under 14 percent alcohol content can be called a Rhine wine.

35. c. They are all sparkling wines, but are not made in the carefully delimited area of France which holds the right to call its wines Champagne.

36. b. To produce these wines, a type of mold, *Botrytis cinerea,* or "noble rot," is needed. This forms on the skin of the grapes, producing the natural sweetness.

37. c. Without the final *s* it is probably American and may be any type of white wine, including very dry. With the final *s* it is French, and refers exclusively to the sweet white wine of the Sauternes district in France. There is no dry Sauternes.

38. c. The delicacies called lobster tails come from

a spiny lobster, like a crayfish, usually found off South America. It is a different species, with small claws, from the North American lobster.

39. a. A man waits until someone catches his eye, then toasts with his glass, maintaining eye contact. *Skoal* or *Skål* means "To your good health." The host may be skoaled, but the hostess never is.

40. a. The women walk behind the headwaiter, or whoever shows you to your seat, and the men walk behind them. If a man is the host, however, he usually goes ahead so that he can point out the seating as the guests reach the table.

41. c. American Plan includes all meals (Modified American Plan provides two meals); European Plan excludes meals. (Continental Plan usually means that morning coffee and rolls are included in the room rate.) In Europe, what we call American Plan is called pension, and two meals a day are called demi-pension.

42. c. There is a rule about this. It is considered incorrect to load your plate with many different kinds of food. Usually it is supposed to be fish first. Next come salads, cold meats, and other cold dishes, and last hot dishes.

43. a. The usual reason is to leave behind the sediment that the wine has "thrown." This is true, usually, only for fine old red wines. (Other wines may be decanted, of course, to create this impression.)

44. c. Mrs. Mary Smith is the form commonly used for divorced women, and is often taken to be an indicator of this status. Ms. is often used to avoid this.

45. c. You never tip an officer on a ship, and a purser is an officer.

46. b. Many people like the saucer shape, especially the kind with a hollow stem so the bubbles rise. Connoisseurs prefer a tulip shape (flute), to keep in the effervescence. (It is considered a waste of good champagne to stir it to remove the bubbles.)

47. a. Any of the dryer ones, but not the cream. In general, except under special circumstances, like serving Sauternes with foie gras, sweet wines are considered undesirable before a meal.

48. c. White before red, lighter before heavier.

49. b. The utensils are set so that you use the ones farthest from the plate first. You take the next in order for each succeeding course.

50. c. It is considered not quite correct to congratulate the lady on having secured a husband. It is entirely appropriate to congratulate the groom on having secured a lovely wife. You just wish the bride happiness.

51. a. None. Announcements are never sent to anyone who has been invited to the wedding, and you may do whatever you want to do.

52. c. There is only one rule. Showers should not be given by the bride's immediate family because a present is obligatory.

53. c. Basically, he should do as much as he can for the groom, taking care of chores like packing, making sure the car (if there is one) is ready to go, and seeing to it that the groom is dressed, has the ring, and so on. As far as the bride is concerned, his major

responsibility is to deliver the groom on time and in a fit condition for the wedding.

54. c. Once upon a time, nothing except the asparagus was finger food. Now the situation is reversed. Asparagus is usually eaten with a fork, and the others may be finger food at home or on a picnic. A hostess considerate of both her guests and her table linen will probably restrict corn on the cob to picnics or very informal meals.

55. a. If it is moving, or if the man can push the door easily, the lady just walks in. Otherwise, she steps in after he starts it. Common sense is the rule here.

Art in the Dark:
Music, Theater, Dance, and Film

1. b. Originally, "tragedy" meant an ode to the *tragos,* or goat, which personified Dionysus. Eventually, several actors told a dramatic story, instead of the ode, but there was still a serious theme.

2. a. Women were not allowed to act on the stage at that time.

3. c. Andrea Palladio, usually considered an architect.

4. a. Sometimes called plain chant, it is apparently the oldest form of church music, unison vocal chanting, not polyphonic.

5. b. Guido of Arezzo. He used four lines. A fifth was added later and the system was in general use by the end of the twelfth century.

6. c. It seems to be a song that we now call "We Won't Go Home Until Morning" or "He's a Jolly Good Fellow." According to most reference works, it was originally sung by the Crusaders.

7. c. At Paris, in the Louvre Palace, in 1581.

8. b. Johann Sebastian Bach (together with hundreds of other compositions).

9. c. Franz Joseph Haydn.

10. b. Wolfgang Amadeus Mozart.

11. b. The harpsichord.

12. a. Jenny Lind.

13. c. *Das Rheingold, Die Walküre, Siegfried,* and *Die Götterdämmerung.*

14. c. Comic opera, as contrasted with serious opera.

15. c. It is a narrative song, usually of popular origin, in which a refrain is repeated after each verse.

16. a. It is a composition for one or two instruments, written in three or four movements. Each movement is distinct from the others in tempo and mood, but similar in style and also in key.

17. c. Lady Macbeth.

18. b. The usual derivation given is from the French *farce*, "stuffing." It started out as an interlude in the main play, for comic relief, and eventually the humorous interlude became a play in itself. Farce was "stuffed" into the original play, according to many sources describing the word's derivation.

19. c. Probably the best-known works are *Oedipus Tyrannus, Oedipus at Colonus, Antigone, Electra, Ajax,* and *Philoctetes.*

20. c. She established a school of dance that is considered to be the forerunner of the modern-dance movement. It was most specifically not classical dancing.

21. c. Called the "Symphony of 1,000," it requires a thousand participants, including singers. It is rarely performed.

22. c. The Barrymores—John, Lionel, and Ethel.

23. c. In general, the operas were performed by a full cast, but had an audience of one—the king.

24. c. Shylock.

25. c. Antoinette Perry, American theater producer (died 1946).

26. c. The title is derived from "immy"—image orthicon, the television camera tube.

27. a. David Wark Griffith.

28. a. Gilbert wrote the words, Sullivan the music.

29. a. Julia Ward Howe.

30. b. Edvard Grieg.

31. a. George S. Kaufman, who also wrote *You Can't Take It with You* and *The Man Who Came to Dinner,* among many others.

32. a. A Russian basso (1873–1938) who was an enormous popular success.

33. c. Minstrels in the south of France in the eleventh to thirteenth centuries, they were musical exponents of the idea of courtly love.

34. a. Franz Lehár, a Hungarian. The operetta's musical celebration of Maxim's made it one of the best-known restaurants in the world.

35. c. Harlequin. Occasionally Pierrot, but he is usually paired with Pierrette.

36. c. Grand Guignol.

37. c. A ship captain accursed for swearing he would round the Cape of Good Hope even if it took an eternity could achieve redemption only if he found a wife willing to sacrifice everything for him.

38. c. Al Jolson.

39. a. New Orleans.

40. b. Vaslav Nijinsky

41. b. The play was *R.U.R.,* or *Rossum's Universal Robots.* If Čapek did not invent the word "robot," he popularized it, and it passed into the literature from this play.

42. a. *Dafne,* written by Jacopo Peri in 1597.

43. c. Aside from *Ah, Wilderness,* a comedy, all of

O'Neill's plays were tragedies, in the true classical sense.

44. c. He wrote several operas, including the immensely popular one known in English as *The Threepenny Opera*.

45. c. Walter Damrosch.

46. b. The composer was watching the bombardment of Ft. McHenry.

47. c. He was the first premier of Poland, for 10 months.

48. c. Kirsten Flagstad, a Norwegian soprano, is fairly generally considered to have been the greatest female singer of Wagner in this century.

49. c. Playacting was not allowed, but representations of scenes in the Bible were frequently acted out during Christmas and Easter masses. These performances moved to the church steps, and then to moving stages, becoming plays. Modern Passion plays are direct descendants of these early dramas.

50. c. In Milan and London respectively.

51. a. We cannot tell the exact year, it seems, but about 1656, the first woman acted in a play called *The Siege of Rhodes*. The fact that boys played women's roles is considered to have been a possible reason for the many cases of girls masquerading as boys, and vice versa, in Shakespeare's plays.

52. c. She played L'Aiglon, the son of Napoleon, a young boy, when she was almost sixty, and apparently was entirely convincing in the role. She also played the title role in *Hamlet* at about the same time, and with equal success.

53. c. Heinrich Heine, a German poet who spent much of his adult life in Paris. The complete works of Heine, one of the best-known German lyric poets, were banned during the Nazi era in Germany, and the song was published as having been written anonymously.

54. c. This is basically the form used in theaters of Shakespeare's time.

55. a. He was the co-founder of the Moscow Art Theater in 1908. His technique of having actors strive for inner interpretations of their roles had a great effect upon theories of acting, and gave his name to this method of interpretation.

Mastering the Highest Cultural Patter: Math and Science

1. a. The second law of thermodynamics states that it is impossible by any continuous self-sustaining process for heat to be transferred from a colder to a hotter body. (This is often given, popularly, as "Heat flows downhill.")

2. c. When mechanical work is transformed into heat, or heat into work, the amount of work is always equivalent to the quantity of heat.

3. b. It was the first time that a provable cause-and-effect relationship had been established for a scientific phenomenon that had previously been considered completely unpredictable and erratic.

4. b. He introduced the concept of the transmission of puerperal (childbed) fever, the idea developed by Semmelweis, and ran a successful campaign to have doctors wash their hands before delivering babies, thus reducing maternal mortality.

5. c. Dr. Alexander Fleming, by accident, in 1928, when a culture was accidentally contaminated with some mold. It was not produced commercially for some time.

6. c. Dr. William Harvey, who published his work in 1628. He was a student at the University of Padua while Galileo was a professor there.

7. a. Carolus Linnaeus, who set up the system basically in use today of classifying plants and animals by a binomial system. (Between 1735 and 1753, he published several works which became the basis for his system of classification.)

8. c. This name is the Latinized form of the Greek Asklepios, the god of medicine and of healing.

9. The first: a. A body remains in a state of rest or uniform motion in a straight line unless compelled by some external force acting upon it to change that state. The second: c. A change in motion is proportional to the force causing the change and takes place in the direction in which the force is acting, or the increase or decrease in velocity is proportional to the force. The third: f. To every action there is always an equal and opposite or contrary reaction.

10. a. It states that the properties of elements are periodic functions of the squares of their atomic numbers. This revision solved the problems of discrepancies in the initial table.

11. c. Leonardo Fibonacci (late 12th–early 13th centuries) demonstrated the sequence in which each number equals the sum of the preceding two numbers: 1 plus 1 equals 2, 1 plus 2 equals 3, 2 plus 3 equals 5, and so on. This arrangement exists in biological forms like the nautilus and the sunflower.

12. b. They won it for their work on radioactivity, and it was awarded in Physics.

13. b. The second Nobel Prize was for the isolation of metallic radium and was awarded in Chemistry.

14. c. Drs. C. F. Cori and Gerty T. Cori, in 1947.

15. c. According to most stories, King Hiero II had asked Archimedes to determine whether a certain crown was made of pure gold, or whether it was alloyed with silver. Archimedes realized that the displacement of metals of different weights would be different. It was the same Hiero II to whom Archime-

des said, regarding the use of a lever, "Give me a place to stand, and I will move the earth."

15. c. *(alternate answer)* Archimedes knew that the densities (weight per unit volume) of different metals were different. Determining the weight of the crown was easy, but determining the volume of the odd-shaped metal was impossible. When he sat in his full bathtub, the water overflowed, and he realized that the volume of water spilled over was equal to the volume of his body in the tub. Eureka! He had a means of determining the volume of an odd shape, and could calculate its density. Then he could compare the density of the crown and of pure gold. (Legend has it that the crown was indeed pure gold.)

16. c. The sum of the squares of the two sides of a right-angled triangle is equal to the square of the hypotenuse.

17. c. This theory deals with the emission and absorption by atoms and by subatomic particles of light and energy, not continuously but in finite steps.

18. a. The Cenozoic era.

19. a. Celsius was Anders Celsius, a Swedish astronomer who invented the centigrade (for 100 divisions) thermometer scale in 1742. Gabriel Fahrenheit was a German physicist who, at about the same time, invented the Fahrenheit thermometer scale. Initially, the centigrade scale froze at 100 and boiled at zero, but this was soon changed.

20. c. It is named after William Thompson, later Lord Kelvin, a British mathematician and physicist. It is considered an "absolute" scale, developed to

start from absolute zero, that point at which molecules of substances have no heat energy.

21. a. It is the measurement of the sides and angles of triangles, particularly the ratios of certain pairs of sides. These ratios and values are called sine, cosine, tangent, cotangent, secant, and cosecant.

22. c. The plate tectonics theory states that land masses are on "plates" which are shifting over and under other plates.

23. a. Geometry is a branch of mathematics which deals with space, the properties of space, and the relations of figures within that space.

24. a. A Greek mathematician named Euclid, who flourished about 300 B.C., set the theorems and problems almost as they exist today, in his book *Elements*. There is also non-Euclidean geometry.

25. a. Geodetic surveying involves distances so large that the curvature of the earth must be taken into account. Two locations a sufficient distance apart are chosen and astronomical methods are used to determine latitude and longitude. Then the baseline, or the distance between the two, is measured. A third station is located by the angle it makes between lines to each of the other two stations, at either end of the baseline. This is called triangulation and is repeated until the entire area is measured and mapped. Plane surveying does not use this method but considers the earth as a horizontal plane.

26. a. This is the branch of mathematics in which the basic operations of mathematics are generalized. In elementary algebra, this is done by the use of

letters to represent numbers. The word itself comes from the Arabic *al-jabr,* meaning "reunion of parts."

27. b. Nicholas Copernicus, a Polish scientist, in his work *De revolutionibus orbium coelestium* (1543), described the sun as the center of a great system, with the earth, one of the planets, revolving around it.

28. a. Galileo accepted the Copernican theory, and published a work of his own on sunspots in 1632. This led to his famous trial, in which he abjured his belief in the Copernican theory. It was at this trial that he is supposed to have said, "Nevertheless, it does move." This famous statement did not appear in accounts of his trial until some two hundred years after the event and cannot be accepted as accurate on the basis of current evidence.

29. c. Blaise Pascal, of France, developed a simple model of an adding machine, using geared wheels, in 1642.

30. c. In 1790, John Fitch ran a passenger steamboat service, at eight miles per hour, between Philadelphia and Burlington, N.J. Even encyclopedias often list his boat as experimental.

31. b. John A. Roebling designed it, but was injured in an accident during the early stages and died. His son, Washington Roebling, supervised the construction. He got caisson disease (probably what is now called "the bends") in 1872, but with the assistance of his wife, Emily, finished the bridge in 1883.

32. a. Joseph and Jacques Montgolfier, French brothers, developed the first manned balloon in

1783. (France had a large celebration in 1983 to mark the anniversary.)

33. b. Thomas A. Edison, in 1870.

34. c. Kepler's third law of planetary motion states that the square of the period is proportional to the cube of the mean distance from the center of gravity of the principal body. In practice, this means that a geosynchronous satellite can be placed only at that one specific distance from the earth.

35. a. The rising and falling sound is the Doppler effect, named after Christian Johann Doppler, who described and explained the phenomenon in 1842. As the distance between a source of wave motion (sound or light, for example) and an observer becomes less or greater, the frequency of the waves received by the observer increases or decreases respectively. In light, this effect is of major importance in measuring the motion of stars.

36. b. They found the "double helix" structure of deoxyribonucleic acid, called DNA, which is the basic building block of cells.

37. a. The X-ray.

38. c. Max Planck, for which he received the Nobel Prize in 1918.

39. c. In 1921, he received the Nobel Prize in Physics for his discovery of the law of the photoelectric effect.

40. a. Dr. Edmund Halley, the second British Astronomer Royal, noted the comet's periodicity in 1682, correlated earlier reports, and predicted that it would appear at approximately 76-year intervals.

He was correct, and on its next appearance, the comet received his name.

41. c. Ladislao Biro, an Argentinian, invented a ballpoint pen that would write on paper, in 1944.

42. c. In 1873, the discovery that there was a variation in the electrical conductivity of selenium when exposed to light produced, simultaneously, a great many early attempts at transmitting pictures. The process did not become practical, however, until the development of the phototube and the mechanical disk scanning method.

43. b. It is Computerized Axial Tomography, a radical new form of X-ray in medicine, which gives pictures of "slices" of the body.

44. c. The invention of holographic three-dimensional imagery.

45. c. The "atomic time clock," which determines the age of objects by measuring the radioactive decay of their components.

46. a. F numbers, or F stops, represent the ratio of the focal length (of the lens) to the effective diameter of the lens. The relative exposure with any two adjacent numbers is in the ratio of one to two. That is, under the same lighting conditions, the larger number admits half as much light and requires an exposure that is twice as long.

47. c. Macadamizing, introduced in England about 1815 by J. L. McAdam, originally utilized compacted layers of small stones. Bituminous macadam roads shortly came into being to "seal" the surface, which otherwise tended to fall apart.

48. c. Bell's telephone used an electric current of fluctuating intensity and frequency, generated by mirroring the acoustic characteristics of sound waves. A thin plate of soft iron, called a diaphragm, vibrated to sound waves just as the eardrum does. Earlier telephones were based on principles that allowed only the transmission of musical pitch without variation in intensity.

49. c. On December 2, 1942, a group working under the direction of Drs. Enrico Fermi and Arthur Compton, at the University of Chicago, produced the first sustained nuclear chain reaction.

50. c. Louis Braille was blinded in an accident when he was three, about 1812. He later developed a system of six raised points or dots in various combinations (63 in all) that makes it possible for the blind to read by touch.

Knowing Whowhatwherewhen
(and when not)

1. a. Akhenaten, who lost his empire as a result. He is known for his monotheism, but is perhaps better remembered as consort to Nefertiti, whose beauty was immortalized in one of the best-known of all sculptures.

2. c. The Etruscans formed a civilization in what is now Italy, mostly northwest of the Tiber, that had reached a high degree of culture prior to the rise of the Romans. Most significantly, their language and culture differed completely from those of the tribes around them, making scholars think they may have come from Asia Minor. Their gold working was the finest of their time, and they may have introduced olive trees and grapes to Italy. They were finally conquered about 400 B.C.

3. c. The Greeks, with 10,000 men, defeated 100,-000 Persians and turned them back, thus ending Persian ambitions of conquest. (The troop numbers are somewhat suspect, especially the Persians'.) The distance run by a messenger carrying news of the victory established the standard for the Marathon run in sports.

4. c. He was King Frederick I of Germany (1121–1190) and the name means "Redbeard." He was a noted warrior, and effected permanent changes in the political alignments of his time, which lasted until fairly recently. Legend has it that he is still sleeping in Thuringia, waiting to rise again.

5. c. The name came from the Latin *provincia,* "the province," and it stuck.

6. c. Although this charter contained very few provisions specifically protecting villeins and tenants, and really was not intended to cover the common man, it did contain the idea that there are laws that the king must obey, which protect the rights of communities and individuals.

7. c. William the Conqueror had a general survey of England made in 1086 to determine the taxable resources of the country. It includes descriptions of all the land and buildings and is invaluable as a source book. The Public Records Office on Chancery Lane in London has a copy of it on exhibit.

8. c. George I could not speak English. He had been elector of Hanover, in Germany, when he became king of England. This lack of English caused some problems. He was a great-grandson of James I, and came to England via the Act of Settlement.

9. c. He appointed an eminent educator, Alcuin, to set up schools and colleges. Alcuin established the liberal arts curriculum that was in use for several hundred years thereafter and, in a slightly modified form, exists in many European universities today.

10. c. The "other" Winston Churchill was an American author who wrote several popular historical novels, which are too often credited to the British Churchill.

11. c. In 1663, the plague struck Oberammergau. A vow was made that if certain dreadful things did not happen, a Passion play would be performed

there. They did not, it was, and it has been every ten years since.

12. a. Siddhartha Gautama (Gotama) flourished between 563 B.C. and 483 B.C.

13. a. Avicenna was a physician. For more than four hundred years, his *Canon of Medicine* was the accepted text in the field.

14. c. Moses ben Maimon, better known as Maimonides.

15. b. Ferdinand and Isabella of Spain. Henry married their daughter, Katharine of Aragon. Henry's daughter, Mary Tudor, married King Philip of Spain, who felt he had a claim to the throne of England when she died, as it had been left to him by Mary, Queen of Scots, in her will. (Mary, Queen of Scots, had disinherited her son in his favor, and as the widower of the queen, he felt he had an additional claim.) He set out with the ill-fated Spanish Armada to claim the throne.

16. c. It is the big city of the Mayan culture, in north central Yucatán, Mexico. It was founded in approximately 514 A.D. and abandoned about 1194.

17. b. Georges Eugène, Baron Haussmann, designed the broad avenues, the beautiful vistas, and the *places,* which are circles with avenues radiating off them. It is claimed that Napoleon III wanted the circles to be thus so that troops could control the radiating avenues by firing in many directions.

18. c. André Lenôtre, who is also believed responsible for the design of the gardens of the Vatican.

19. b. The technique of working with the clay that produces fine bone china, and with the bone used for strengthening the china, was developed here. Wedgwood, Spode, Minton, and many other world-famous firms have their factories in this area.

20. c. The French Ministry of Foreign Affairs, whose building stands on the Quai d'Orsay.

21. b. Iceland actually means "Island," which it most certainly is. The North Atlantic Drift is responsible for the mildness of the climate.

22. c. A chain of active volcanoes stretches around the Pacific Ocean, from Alaska in the north down to the tip of South America, and up through New Zealand and Japan.

23. a. Captain Dreyfus was completely exonerated in 1906, given the Legion of Honor, and made a major. He served with honor in World War I, rising to the rank of general. He lived long enough to see himself completely cleared in 1930, by the publication of the papers of Major Max von Schwartzkoppen, to whom the alleged treasonous schedule had been written.

24. c. Florenz Ziegfeld, in the *Follies of 1907*.

25. c. Friedrich Engels, upon the death of Marx. Incidentally, Marx wrote most of his material in the British Museum and is buried in London.

26. b. These are laws limiting the use of certain clothing, jewelry, or foods to a particular class, usually to prevent the lower classes from "showing off." They date back to Roman times, existed in the Mid-

dle Ages, and continued until fairly recently. Their chief effect was to make the forbidden fruit even sweeter.

27. c. Blue laws was a term apparently coined by Reverend Samuel A. Peters. Criticized for his nonconformism in Connecticut, he fled in 1744 to England, where he wrote a book describing the laws that restricted personal morality. The term stuck and American laws circumscribing personal actions on a moral basis are still called that. (An example would be a ban on store sales on Sunday.)

28. a. Count Ferdinand von Zeppelin, a German aeronautical pioneer, made the first rigid airship in 1900.

29. c. On June 28, 1914, Archduke Francis Ferdinand, heir to Emperor Franz Joseph, was assassinated at Sarajevo. It took several weeks for all of Europe to get involved, but by September 4, most European countries were engaged in the war.

30. b. This was a mighty system of fortifications along the French border from Switzerland to the Belgian border. It proved useless to the French during the war.

31. a. Marshal Pétain, who set his government up at Vichy, in southern France.

32. c. Korea basically was ruled by China from the eighteenth century until 1910, when it was formally taken over by Japan. It was called Chosen.

33. b. This battle marked the high point of the Muslim invasion of Europe. They were never able to

get any farther north than this, about 100 miles from Paris, and retreated to the Iberian Peninsula, from which the last remnants were driven at the time of Columbus.

34. c. He was a signer of the Declaration of Independence, whose signature is one of the most valuable, as it is extremely rare.

35. a. The division of Berlin was agreed upon, and Russia agreed to enter the war against Japan within three months of Germany's surrender. There were many other provisions.

36. b. This act established the system of land-grant colleges for higher education, a total of sixty-nine colleges and universities which generally represent not only the older state systems, but also the universities of Alaska, Hawaii, and Puerto Rico.

37. c. He was a Stuart claimant to the British throne, the grandson of James II. Parliament had passed an act removing his father from the right of succession, and Bonnie Prince Charlie, a romantic hero, but apparently not much of a soldier, led a rebellion which was defeated, with great loss of life, at Culloden, in Scotland.

38. c. Washington was a British officer in the French and Indian Wars.

39. c. Grigori Aleksandrovich Potemkin was alleged to have built false fronts to represent thriving villages along the routes followed by Catherine the Great of Russia. This was done, it was said, to give her a false impression of success. A "Potemkin village" is a sham.

40. c. He was born in New York in 1882, and taken to Ireland as a child.

41. b. James T. Brudenell was the Seventh earl of Cardigan, and is probably best remembered for the type of jacket he wore, still called a cardigan.

42. c. John Dewey, chiefly associated with Columbia University. He is often blamed for excesses that had little or nothing to do with his actual ideas.

43. a. Paterson, although he lived in Rutherford, New Jersey.

44. c. Hemophilia: the heir to the Russian throne suffered from it, and so did several of the Spanish princes.

45. b. Hoover was a mining engineer, and a very successful one.

46. c. At Jamestown, Virginia, in 1607, on the site of an abandoned Spanish settlement called San Miguel, settled in 1526.

47. b. William the Conqueror, who built a chain of such "command posts" all over his conquered territories.

48. c. A submarine, powered by an electric motor, and commissioned by the U.S. Navy in 1900.

49. a. He was the descendant of the Norsemen who took over Normandy—the land of the Nor(s)men—in 911. He was only one hundred years removed from his Viking ancestors. Duke Rollo, the original Viking conqueror of Normandy, died in 931, and William is believed to have been born in 1027, his great-grandson.

50. c. Iceland. It does not seem to have native

inhabitants and was settled by Scandinavians, who had a long tradition of literacy.

51. c. He crossed the Alps with a complete baggage train and a retinue of elephants.

52. b. He found the buried site of Troy. A German who made most of his fortune in Russia, he was also an American citizen because he happened to be living in California when it became a state.

53. b. It is the Donau in German, and the song's title sounds more musical in its original language— "Blau Donau."

54. c. It is an inlet of the Bosporus at Istanbul, and is considered to be one of the most beautiful water sites in the world.

55. c. This is one of the largest geologic fault systems in the world, running roughly from latitude 35° North to latitude 20° South. The northern extension runs through Syria down into the Red Sea, and branches into the Gulf of Aden. The main body of the rift runs down from the Red Sea across Ethiopia and then south across Africa to West Mozambique. It varies from 1,300 feet below sea level on the floor of the Dead Sea to over 6,000 feet high in the mountains.

For the Cultural Elite Only

1. c. It is from the Latin word for "joy," *io.* The word was eventually abbreviated by placing the *i* on top and the *o* underneath, finally appearing as *!*

2. a. Legend, and the tour guides in the champagne cellars in Rheims, France, indicate that Marie Antoinette was so proud of her beautiful breasts that she had this glass shape modeled on them.

3. a. "I count none but sunny hours," or some variation of that. The Latin is: *Horas non numero nisi serenas.*

4. c. The Huang He River, in China, flooded in August 1931. As far as can be determined, 3,700,000 people drowned.

5. b. English is not considered a Romance language. Both Rumanian and Portuguese are thus classified.

6. b. In a fit of emotion, he had placed it in the coffin of his wife, whom he dearly loved, and who died shortly after their marriage.

7. b. Goldfish are a developed species of carp. In China there is a similar fish, of a dark color. Goldfish can also change color and their size is partly dependent upon their environment.

8. c. The arrangement at 8:18 is symmetrical, pleasing to the eye, and offers a large amount of unobstructed advertising space. It has nothing to do with Lincoln's death, which occurred at about 7:30 A.M.

9. b. In some countries there is also a bucket, a symbol of catching the blood. A blue stripe was added in the U.S.

10. c. The Duke used to play the game with a tennis ball, in the house, and was persuaded, probably by his accountant, that a shuttlecock would be better.

11. a. Few people use it in this way now.

12. c. Despite all the claims, nothing has been conclusively proved.

13. b. The cult was wiped out by the British in the nineteenth century.

14. b.

15. a. And vice versa south of the equator.

16. b.

17. c. Harriet Beecher Stowe, author of *Uncle Tom's Cabin.* It was Lincoln who named her thus.

18. b. As far as we know. Anything like this is subject to revision by historians.

19. c.

20. c. All of them were born before the United States became a nation, so all were technically born in a British colony. Martin Van Buren was our first President to be born after the United States had become a nation.

Rating Your C.Q. (a must!)

Once you've taken the test, add up your score for all of the chapters (there are 55 possible points for each chapter, and 22 for the "Cultural Elite" quiz), and check your score against the ratings shown below. The total number of right answers is the equivalent of your Culture Quotient. Then—if you've done well —fill in your very own CULTURE QUOTIENT CARD as provided, and remove it (artfully, of course) from the book. Show it around! Carry it in your wallet! Be the proud owner of your very own CULTURE QUOTIENT SCORE! It will make all the difference to the people you meet at the best parties.

SCORING:

150 and above—CULTURAL GENIUS

Congratulations! (Are you sure this is an honest count?) If you scored more than 24 right answers and less than 40 in each category, you may safely discuss anything at cocktail parties, vernissages, and the like. As a matter of fact, you will probably find that things get even better as the time passes and the bottles empty. *Facile Princeps* (or, "easily first.")

130 to 149—ENORMOUSLY SUPERIOR

(Again, check your category scores.) If you have more than 40 right answers in any one category, you may well make others feel miserably inferior when sharing your knowledge of that category. Steer clear of discussions in any subject in which you achieved a score of less than 20. You may well find it a bit like going a few rounds with Joe Louis.

110 to 129—EXCEPTIONALLY ACCEPTABLE

While you still can hold your own in any gathering, you should master a few of the cultural ploys noted in the introduction to each section. As for the areas in which you did least well, you might want to do a little brushing up (perhaps a lot of brushing up), if not on the facts, then certainly on the ploys.

90 to 109—RATHER RESPECTABLE

Very good, but no Distinguished Culture Medals. Your best technique would probably be to look wise, and drop into your conversation one of the more obscure items of information where appropriate, but refuse to let yourself be drawn further into the con-

versation. This should gain you a reputation for deep
thought.

Below 90—NICE BUT TERRIBLY AVERAGE

If you score below 90, you might just keep your ears
open and maintain that silence is golden. Of course,
if anyone remarks on your nonparticipation, explain
that you are an observer that evening, or murmur, in
Latin, *"Aurum silentium,"* which translates neatly
into "Silence is golden," but sounds more chic this
way.

_____
NAME

is the proud bearer

of a C.Q. of _____